Pause, Ponder, and Persist in the Classroom

How can educators find joy in the midst of seemingly overwhelming challenges? Researcher Julie Schmidt Hasson interviewed hundreds of people about their most impactful teachers and shares her findings in this unique and powerful book. She lays out a three-step process that leads to greater peace, and greater impact on students.

This three-step framework involves pausing, pondering, and persisting. First, teachers pause before reacting to an unexpected challenge, so they can intentionally choose a response. Next, they suspend assumptions and approach the challenge from a place of curiosity. Finally, they persist in this dance of patient inquiry and thoughtful responses in a way that leads to better outcomes for students.

The stories integrated throughout the book provide evidence of the many ways teachers make a difference in students' lives. It is a challenging time to be a teacher, and this book provides the inspiration and information teachers need to stay longer, grow stronger, and continue making an impact.

Julie Schmidt Hasson, Ed.D. (@JulieSHasson) is a professor in the Reich College of Education at Appalachian State University. Julie's research on the impact of a teacher is the topic of a TEDx talk and is the focus of her engaging professional development programs. She founded the Chalk and Chances project, a vehicle for elevating and celebrating teachers, in 2017.

T0386472

Pause, Ponder, and Persist in the Classroom

How Teachers Turn Challenges into Opportunities for Impact

Julie Schmidt Hasson

Routledge
Taylor & Francis Group

NEW YORK AND LONDON

First published 2023
by Routledge
605 Third Avenue, New York, NY 10158

and by Routledge
4 Park Square, Milton Park, Abingdon, Oxon, OX14 4RN

Routledge is an imprint of the Taylor & Francis Group, an informa business

© 2023 Julie Schmidt Hasson

Library of Congress Cataloging-in-Publication Data
Names: Schmidt Hasson, Julie, author.
Title: Pause, ponder, and persist in the classroom:
how teachers turn challenges into opportunities for
impact / Julie Schmidt Hasson.
Description: New York, NY: Routledge, 2023. |
Includes bibliographical references.
Identifiers: LCCN 2022057149 | ISBN 9781032383774 (hardback) |
ISBN 9781032383422 (paperback) | ISBN 9781003344735 (ebook)
Subjects: LCSH: Classroom management. |
Effective teaching. | Teacher-student relationships.
Classification: LCC LB3013 .S3467 2023 |
DDC 371.102/4—dc23/eng/20230126
LC record available at https://lccn.loc.gov/2022057149

ISBN: 978-1-032-38377-4 (hbk)
ISBN: 978-1-032-38342-2 (pbk)
ISBN: 978-1-003-34473-5 (ebk)

DOI: 10.4324/9781003344735

Typeset in Palatino
by codeMantra

To Brian, whose journey in teaching inspires me

Contents

Acknowledgements

Bringing a book to life is a collaborative process. I am grateful to Lauren Davis and the team at Routledge/Taylor and Francis Group for helping to transform my words into a beautiful book. Thank you to Caite Hamilton for shaping this work and carefully polishing each paragraph.

I've been blessed with unwavering support from my family and friends. Thank you to Brian Hasson for being a partner in every sense of the word and to Cailin Hasson for helping me look at teaching with fresh eyes. Thank you to Laura Estes-Swilley for four decades of friendship and for the hundreds of conversations about what it means to live this teaching life.

Every child deserves to be nurtured as I was (and continue to be). Thank you to my parents, Bob and Gayle Schmidt, who always believed I could be a writer and who proudly displayed every piece on the refrigerator. Thank you to Mrs. Nancy Russell, who encouraged me when I was an emerging reader and again when I was an emerging leader.

I've been lucky enough to spend most of my life surrounded by educators. Thank you to all of the teachers who ignited my love of learning, to my colleagues who keep that fire burning, and to my students who provide my why. Most importantly, thank you to teachers everywhere for making the world a better place by making students feel safe, seen, and stretched every day.

Meet the Author

Dr. Julie Hasson is a professor in the Reich College of Education at Appalachian State University. When Julie is not teaching graduate classes in school leadership, she is conducting qualitative research in schools. Julie's research on the impact of a teacher is the topic of a TEDx talk and is the focus of her engaging professional development programs. She founded the Chalk and Chances project, a vehicle for elevating and celebrating teachers, in 2017. She is also the author of *Unmapped Potential: An Educator's Guide to Lasting Change* (2017) and *Safe, Seen, and Stretched in the Classroom: The Remarkable Ways Teachers Shape Students' Lives* (2022). She lives in Boone, North Carolina, with her husband, two dogs, and several geese.

Introduction

Teaching … No other profession has higher highs or lower lows. The work is undeniably complex and challenging. Why do teachers stay? For most, it's the deep satisfaction that comes from impacting the lives of students. However, opportunities for impact rarely present themselves in moments of wonder and delight. More often, these opportunities come hidden in a challenge or problem. The ability to not just navigate through a problem but to turn that problem into an opportunity for impact is the hallmark of a life-shaping teacher. How do teachers push past the busyness of the day to intentionally find the potential in a problem? In my yearlong quest to answer this question, I interviewed former students about their most impactful teachers. I also interviewed and observed teachers in action to identify common practices.

In my previous book, *Safe, Seen, and Stretched in the Classroom: The Remarkable Ways Teachers Shape Students' Lives*, I shared data collected by asking hundreds of people about the teachers they remember. In the stories former students shared about turning points in their lives, teachers often paused in the midst of a difficult situation. When a student's words or behaviors initiated unhelpful emotions, these teachers paused and took a breath. It's natural to feel frustrated or angry when a disrespectful remark or action interrupts a lesson, but a hasty reaction fueled by emotions can make a situation worse. Words spoken in anger can also damage a relationship. For teachers who consistently make an impact, the pause is a safeguard, preventing a regrettable reaction. A pause helps everyone in the classroom community feel safe.

It's not typically the situation itself that stirs emotions, it's the stories or interpretations attached to it. Therefore, following

DOI: 10.4324/9781003344735-1

a pause, the life-shaping teachers in the former students' stories took a curious stance. They pushed aside assumptions about the thoughts and intentions behind the actions, and instead, asked questions. They pondered, humbly inquiring about the student's perspective. No one likes to be the subject of misjudgment or faulty assumptions, but genuine curiosity helps students feel seen.

The most impactful teachers also demonstrated a high degree of persistence, especially when teaching students who struggle to learn or have challenging behaviors. It's tempting to think that having talent or excellent training is the key to great teaching, but even the most solid foundational skills won't take teachers far without persistence. It is through trial and error, reflection, and skill building that teachers learn to adapt their teaching for a diverse group of students with a variety of needs. What works with one student or one class may not work with others. Persisting is what allows students and teachers to stretch.

Examples of pausing, pondering, and persisting are evident throughout the stories I collected, and this three-step framework can lead to greater impact and also greater satisfaction for teachers. In order to arrive at the framework, I used a grounded theory approach to data collection and analysis, simultaneously collecting, coding, and analyzing data from my interviews and field notes. I did not purposefully select participants for the study. Instead, I placed myself where I was likely to find a diversity of backgrounds and perspectives. I made no assumptions about the race, ethnicity, gender, economic status, or ability of the participants. In some cases, information about these identities was shared in their stories.

The book you are holding represents a synthesis of the findings after the first year of the project. The names of some of the participants (and other identifying information) have been changed to protect confidentiality. In some cases, the timeline was compressed and events reordered to assist the reader in following the narrative. It is important to note that all memories are reconstructions. The stories people tell are filtered through their current realities. The meaning given to a story is influenced by the events that have transpired since the experience. I have reported the stories as they were told to me (with a bit of editing for readability). I have reported the events to the best of my recollection, with support from my field notes.

In the pages of this book, I situated my findings in the context of existing research on teaching and learning. My goal was to create a work grounded in evidence but also accessible to teachers. And so, in addition to the content in each chapter, I also included tools for implementation and reflection questions (which may be incorporated into a book study). I continually find myself straddling two worlds, with one foot in the scholarly realm and the other foot in the classroom. This research has deepened my affinity for teachers and their profession. This work has affirmed my belief that teachers have the power to shape students' lives, and they do so in a million different ways every day. The seemingly ordinary actions and interactions that occur in classrooms have extraordinary implications. It is my hope that this framework of pausing, pondering, and persisting can help teachers stay longer, grow stronger, and continue making an impact.

1

The Power of a Problem

In countless ways every day, teachers have opportunities to impact students' lives. But these opportunities don't always present themselves as welcome occasions. Often, they come disguised as challenges or problems. The ability to not just navigate through a problem but to turn that problem into an opportunity for impact is the hallmark of a life–shaping teacher. When unexpected challenges happen in the classroom, impactful teachers somehow see the hidden potential for their students' growth and their own development. I was thinking about this capacity to turn a problem into an opportunity as I packed jars of peanut butter in boxes. I knew if I could figure out how teachers do this, I could more intentionally and consistently look for opportunities when problems surface in my own life. And the pandemic had brought a myriad of difficulties for me to navigate. After months spent in pandemic remoteness, I longed to engage with my community again. That's what led me to volunteer at the food bank. And so, instead of packing my schedule with more Zoom meetings, today I was packing peanut butter.

As I worked, I thought about the current reality for teachers. I knew my own pandemic challenges as a professor and researcher paled in comparison to the challenges of K-12 teachers. Most faced a quick pivot from in person to remote teaching with very little time to prepare. While balancing their own needs and the needs of their families, they still managed to attend to the academic, social, and emotional needs of their students.

DOI: 10.4324/9781003344735-2

Many months later, as things stabilized a bit, educators thought that feeling of pandemic-related burnout might ease. However, unrealistic expectations have continued to drive many teachers out of the profession. This became clear to me in a recent conversation with a former graduate student. Deanna (one of the most effective and dedicated teachers I know) called to tell me she was considering leaving teaching. Her words still echo in my mind. "It's not that teaching has become harder," she said, "It's just become the wrong kind of hard."

Teaching has always been difficult. Trying to meet the varying needs of a diverse group of young people takes incredible skill and commitment. In the past, feeling overwhelmed was more typical for those new to the profession. Feeling burned out was most prevalent in veterans who were asked to take on too many extra responsibilities. But recently, feelings of overwhelm and fatigue are commonly reported by teachers at all levels of experience. Systemic issues have caused many to lose hope and opt for a different career. Others choose to stay and try to continue making an impact, despite the toll it takes on their own well-being. As I worked at the table in the food bank, I thought about those teachers who stay. Could the way teachers respond to challenges make the difference between lighting up and burning out? And if so, what are the steps to a helpful response in the face of a challenge?

An Opportunity for Impact

I appreciated the time to ponder that the repetitive task of packing jars provided. Still, I was happy when Marcus (a regular volunteer at the food bank) arrived at the packing table to help. Like most strangers meeting for the first time, we chatted about our work. Marcus revealed that he directed the marketing department at a new technology company, while I shared my experience as a professor, teaching graduate students and conducting research. I told him about my quest to understand what teachers say and do to make a lasting impact on their students' lives and confessed that after years of exploring teacher impact, I'm still trying to figure it out. Whenever I explain my research to someone new, I am typically blessed with a story about a favorite teacher, and Marcus was no exception.

"Mrs. Pope was my home economics teacher," he began, dragging a tape gun from one side of a box to the other. "I loved her class because of her kindness—and because we often cooked. One day, we made chocolate chip cookies. After they cooled, Mrs. Pope said we could each eat one. I snuck three more in my pocket." Marcus realized his teacher must have seen him when she asked him to stay after class.

"I expected Mrs. Pope to lecture me or to write me a referral. Instead, she just asked, 'Are you hungry?' I told her that my dad left a few months ago, and my mom wasn't doing well. I told her that our electricity had been off for a while."

Marcus noticed his teacher gaze down at the spots on his shirt, then she did something he didn't expect. She offered to let him wash his clothes in the washing machine housed in the home economics classroom.

"I brought my clothes by the next morning," he recalled. "When I came back to get them, they were carefully folded, and they smelled so good. Next to my clothes was a large, brown bag with my name written on it. I peeked in the bag and found bread, peanut butter, cans of soup, and other snacks."

Marcus leaned on the boxes. "Throughout my high school years, Mrs. Pope checked on me. My clothes were washed in that home economics classroom more times than I could count. My teacher and the ladies in her church group were the only reason I ate most nights." Marcus told me that Mrs. Pope is gone now, and he can't repay her for the kindness, but he tries to pay it forward by volunteering in our local food pantry.

My new friend and I talked about what it's like to be hungry and shared our gratitude for teachers like Mrs. Pope. We quietly blessed the boxes we had packed and hoped they would help kids struggling the way Marcus had. Then we signed out on the volunteer sheet, put on our coats, and walked into the cold evening air. "It's the wind that gets you up here!" Marcus shouted as he headed toward his car.

Faulty Assumptions

Brian (my husband) and I moved to the mountains of Western North Carolina two years ago to become faculty members at Appalachian State University. I was getting more accustomed to the curvy roads, but I still tried to get home before dark. On the way, I reflected on Marcus's story. It was a beautiful example of turning a problem into an opportunity for impact. When Mrs. Pope saw Marcus take the extra cookies, her initial reaction was surely frustration or anger, especially since she had given clear directions. How did she push past that initial reaction and, instead, respond with compassion?

What struck me most about the story was the teacher's decision to ask a question rather than assume. I considered how differently his story may have ended if Marcus's teacher had responded based on assumptions she'd made. She may have assumed Marcus was greedy, or disrespectful, or worse. She may have written an office referral or excluded him from future cooking projects. Those decisions may have been justified, but they would have created a great divide in her relationship with Marcus and would have made things even more difficult for an already struggling kid. Yes, it's important to hold students accountable for their actions, but it's helpful to know the story behind those actions first. We are right to expect students to follow directions, but do we want to focus on being right or on making an impact? If Mrs. Pope had focused on being right, she would have missed the opportunity to make a positive impact on the life of a student, one who would continue to honor her years later.

I also thought about what I would have missed if I hadn't heard Marcus' story. I'm an introvert, but I rarely regret pushing past my discomfort to engage in a conversation with a stranger.

I have, however, read enough news stories to know that encounters with strangers can go terribly wrong. Author and journalist Malcolm Gladwell examined the varying ways we misinterpret or fail to communicate with one another, particularly with strangers. In his book, *Talking to Strangers: What We Should Know About People We Don't Know*, he cautions against making assumptions when someone's actions don't conform to our own norms. The tools and strategies we use to interpret the words and actions of people we don't know are often flawed. We can easily create inaccurate narratives about the intentions of others, and we are even more likely to misunderstand one another when we come from different cultures or backgrounds. These misunderstandings can lead to conflict, and the outcome can be harmful. This is particularly true for people in positions of power, like teachers. Making an effort to know our students is critical because our misunderstandings can lead to choices that have a detrimental impact on their lives.

Digging Deeper

I made it into the valley, down our gravel road, and into my home office just in time to begin a remote meeting with a group of eight doctoral students. This group of emerging scholars is focused on successfully navigating the dissertation process. During our weekly meetings, we update each other on our writing productivity and talk about our challenges. Their dedication and enthusiasm inspire me to continue my own research, and they are helpful sounding boards. My students knew that I'd been digging deeper into my data on teacher impact, thinking there was more to be revealed. I just couldn't quite put my finger on it yet.

As a professor and educational researcher, I explore the ways teachers influence the academic, social, and emotional outcomes of their students. I'm a qualitative researcher, which means I collect data through observations and interviews, rather than hard numbers. Initially inspired by my own teachers, I set out to understand the lasting impact teachers make on our lives. For the past five years, I've interviewed people who were once students in schools (which is almost everyone). I visited farmers markets, craft fairs, and public parks with a sign that said, *Let's chat about a teacher you remember,* and hundreds of people shared their stories with me. Sitting at the park with a sign is not a typical data collection method, but it was the best crazy idea I've ever had.

Using a grounded theory approach, I analyzed the stories people shared (and my own field notes) line by line in order to identify emerging categories and themes. It became clear that what people remember most about their teachers is the way those teachers made them feel. Over and over again, people described feeling safe, seen, and stretched in their favorite teachers' classrooms. When teachers created a safe space for students, those students could show up fully as themselves and be seen. Then, teachers gently pushed them toward their potential. They helped them stretch. I wrote about the life-shaping power of teachers in *Safe, Seen, and Stretched in the Classroom: The Remarkable Ways Teachers Shape Students' Lives*, but now I was wondering how teachers recognize opportunities for impact. When an unexpected challenge happens in the classroom, how do they turn that problem into an opportunity?

Seeking to Understand

In our Zoom meeting, I asked my students if they had ever experienced a moment that could have been painful or regrettable, but instead turned into a positive experience because of a teacher's response. Daniella thought her experience with Mr. Avery might provide some insight.

"The day after my 16th birthday, my father was diagnosed with cancer," she began, her voice shaking a little. "It was aggressively moving into his bones, and he had to begin intense treatment right away. My family never had much in the way of financial resources, but we got by. When my father had to stop working, it was devastating. I managed to pick up two after school jobs. I babysat until dinner time. After that, I went straight to my waitressing job. I got home around midnight and then tried to catch up on my homework and studying." Daniella had always been a good student but was finding it hard to keep her grades up.

"I loved Mr. Avery's history class," she continued. "He made the subject come alive and he was always enthusiastic, so I was mortified to find myself suddenly awakened by the bell at the end of his class one day. Before I could pull myself together and collect my things, all of the other students had left. I had to face Mr. Avery. I was afraid he would think I didn't care about his class. Or worse, he might think I was partying or abusing alcohol or drugs."

Daniella recalled walking up to her teacher's desk. "Mr. Avery said he'd noticed a change in me, that lately I wasn't engaged in class. He asked what had happened to cause such a change." Daniella decided to tell him about her father. She told him how she needed to work to help support her family. "I apologized for falling asleep. He just listened and reassured me that he wasn't disappointed."

When Daniella got home from her waitressing job that night, her mother was waiting up. Mr. Avery had called. He wanted to refer the family to an organization that could assist them.

"Because of Mr. Avery's support, we received food and help with medical bills. I was able to work less hours, and my parents were able to feel a sense of peace," Daniella shared. "I will never forget his willingness to go above and beyond his teaching responsibilities to help a tired kid and a family in need."

We all agreed that Daniella's story provided insight into the ways teachers like Mr. Avery turn a potentially dubious situation into an opportunity to make an impact. He could have taken offense at her falling asleep. He could have assumed she was disinterested and lazy, and therefore, chosen not to invest in her success. Instead, he asked a question. There was definitely something interesting about a teacher's ability to thwart an initial emotion driven reaction and suspend judgment in an effort to understand. I thanked my students for helping me dig deeper into the idea. After everyone got the assistance and support needed to keep writing, I clicked the red leave button and closed my laptop.

Being Other Focused

The research of psychologist John Gottman has an undeniable influence on my understanding of student–teacher interactions. Although he mainly studies romantic relationships, his findings are broadly applicable. Dr. Gottman has identified bids for connection as the building blocks of relationships. A bid is an attempt to gain attention, affirmation, affection, or any other positive connection from another person. Relationships are built by consistently noticing and responding to bids. There is ample evidence in my data that this holds true for student–teacher relationships.

When a student gives a bid for connection, we can respond in three ways. We can turn against, turn away, or turn toward. Turning against means responding in a demeaning or critical manner. It can easily happen when we are frustrated. For example, if a student is crying, responding by calling the student dramatic would be turning against. Turning away is giving no response at all. It often happens when we are preoccupied and not focused on the other person. The response best for building relationships, turning toward, entails responding in a caring, affirming way. Consoling the crying student and inquiring about what's wrong is turning toward, which provides the care and connection the student is seeking.

I finished my cup of tea and opened my journal. I was wondering about bids for connection and how they precede moments of impact in the classroom. How do our responses to bids for connection determine the kind of impact we make, for better or worse? How do teachers like Mrs. Pope and Mr. Avery, teachers who make positive and consequential differences in students' lives, respond to unexpected or challenging events? Perhaps students aren't always intentionally sending bids, but their actions indicate a need for help. When a student sneaks extra cookies or falls asleep, how do the most impactful teachers respond? What can we learn from them? I quickly jotted down these questions.

Realizing I needed more examples, I rifled through my data file and pulled out a stack of stories. I found my transcription of a story shared by a young woman named Shelby. I met Shelby on a college campus where she was pursuing a graduate degree in social work. She was full of energy, practically bouncing as she shared her memory of her fourth grade teacher, Mrs. Berns.

"I loved going to Mrs. Berns' classroom," she started. "It was a peaceful sanctuary in my otherwise chaotic young life. I was always well behaved in school. However, I felt like an annoyance to my teachers—until I met Mrs. Berns." Shelby described her childhood self as scattered, constantly losing or forgetting things. She recalled the teachers prior to Mrs. Berns becoming annoyed by her missing papers and library books. "Just a few weeks into my fourth grade year," Shelby continued, "Mrs. Berns noticed that I had not turned in homework for several days. I was ready for her to lecture me, but instead she asked me questions: "Do you have a quiet place to do your homework after school? What is your after-school time like?"

Shelby explained that she usually went to one of her aunt's houses because her mom had to work. Sometimes she went to her grandma's house. She never really knew where she would end up. "I went with the relative who could take me," she said. "If my mom worked late, I slept at a relative's house. This happened more often than not, so my belongings were always scattered all over the place, and never where I needed them."

Shelby recalled feeling a little embarrassed telling her teacher about her situation. "Mrs. Berns stood there for a minute, then she walked over and cleared off a little desk by the window. She placed some paper and a box of pencils on the desk. She told me to pick up my breakfast and come directly to my new home-work spot instead of waiting for the morning bell with the other kids." Shelby smiled as she described how she worked on her homework every morning and kept her library books and other important things inside the desk. "The routine was comforting, and I treasured the extra time with my teacher." Mrs. Berns could have let her frustration drive her reaction to Shelby's missing work. Instead, she asked questions. This teacher made a lasting impact by finding out what her student needed and figuring out a way to provide it.

Relational Care

Shelby's story offered a beautiful example of a teacher push-ing past the urge to react in frustration and respond with grace instead. By doing so, Mrs. Berns demonstrated relational care. Educator and philosopher Nel Noddings is known for her work around the ethic of care, and according to Dr. Noddings, caring is grounded in intention and attention. It is a focus on another while (explicitly or implicitly) asking, *What are you going through?* A caring teacher is receptive, trying to understand what the stu-dent is experiencing. From the perspective of the ethic of care, the teacher as carer is interested in the expressed needs of the stu-dent, not simply the needs assumed by the teacher or the school. As the teacher inquires and receives information from the stu-dent, the student feels recognized. In other words, focused and caring inquiry helps the student feel seen and valued.

After listening, the caring teacher then decides how to respond and, if possible, responds directly to the student's expressed need. But, if helping the student to solve the problem is not possible (at least not in the moment), the caring teacher still responds in a way that strengthens the relationship. There are many times when teachers cannot satisfy the expressed need of the student. Perhaps we lack the resources or feel it crosses a boundary. For example, a teacher may not be able to directly intervene when a student is experiencing conflict at home. It is then especially important to find a way of responding that still validates the student's needs. Just the willingness to listen and desire to help can communicate the teacher's valuing of the student and the relationship. Mrs. Berns couldn't reduce the chaos in Shelby's home life, but through her caring response, she could provide a sense of calm at school.

A Mindful Pause

This is the point where I must acknowledge that teachers are human, and what challenges humans more than anything else is other humans. Teachers interact with 20 or more humans all day, every day. To add a degree of difficulty, they interact with those whose brains are not yet fully formed. I've spent more than 30 years as an educator and parent, and I carry countless recollections of regrettable moments when words tumbled out of my mouth that I immediately wished could be reeled back in. Luckily, there have also been times when I responded in thoughtful ways. What made the difference between helping and harming? There was one thing present in all of the helpful responses and absent in all of the hasty reactions: a pause. Pausing and taking a breath seemed to be the safeguard, the barrier that kept regrettable words from escaping.

Psychologist Shauna Shapiro calls this practice "mindful pausing." According to Dr. Shapiro, a moment of pause between an event and a response can make all the difference. But this is easier said than done. The limbic system, which controls our emotions, is typically the first to respond in a stressful situation, causing us to react automatically and quickly instead of slowly and thoughtfully. But a pause gives the reasoning prefrontal cortex time to get started. A pause gives us the space to see a situation clearly and choose a response, rather than automatically reacting in ways that may not serve us, others, or the situation. When we pause in mindfulness, we take a step back from whatever is happening in order to observe a situation more objectively. A mindful pause puts us back in control.

Pausing also allows us to become aware of our thoughts. What story are we telling ourselves about the situation? What assumptions are we making about the other person? In the heat of the moment, it's easy to make assumptions about someone else's intentions or the meaning behind their actions. Pausing allows us to consider other options. Is a student acting inappropriately just to aggravate the teacher, or is it possible the student lacks the ability to self-regulate? What else could be going on? What do we not know that may shed some light on the situation? Pausing and questioning our quickly contrived narratives seem key to responding to challenges in ways that create a positive impact.

Slowing Down

One of my favorite movie characters, Ferris Bueller, once said, "Life moves pretty fast. If you don't stop and look around once in a while, you could miss it." The classroom is a fast-paced environment. If we're not intentional in our focus, we can easily miss the small moments that become opportunities for big impact. If we react to events rather than thoughtfully responding, we can do harm. I decided that slowing down, paying attention, and pausing might just be the path to finding a greater sense of peace and making a more consistent impact. Teaching is full of challenges, and the way we respond to those challenges determines the kind of impact we will make. And, the way we deal with challenges in the classroom can either light us up or burn us out.

By the time I turned off my office light, my journal pages overflowed with questions: What happens in the mind of a teacher between an unexpected challenge in the classroom and a response? Could pausing and seeking to understand in a difficult moment increase the likelihood of positively impacting a student's life? Most importantly, does choosing the path more likely to make an impact add to a teacher's sense of satisfaction? Wrestling with these questions would have to wait. I needed some sleep because tomorrow I was heading to Briarwood Elementary, where I had been coaching Sarah Ross, a new principal. I planned to shadow her throughout the day, and I couldn't help but wonder if I would find more examples of turning problems into opportunities for impact at Briarwood.

 ## Leveraging the Power of a Problem

Pausing with a Problem

The first step in finding the opportunities hidden in problems is to accept that problems are an inevitable part of daily life, especially in the classroom. Technology will have glitches, schedules will change, and students will behave in unpredictable ways. Expecting challenges can keep you from being thrown off course when they occur. When a problem arises, take a breath. A pause gives you the chance to identify your own emotions. An unexpected challenge likely produces initial feelings of frustration, overwhelm, or anger. A pause provides the space to quiet a rising emotionally driven reaction in favor of a more thoughtful response.

Pondering about a Problem

The second step in turning challenges into opportunities for impact is avoiding the creation of an initial narrative about the problem. Our first reaction to a problem is typically negative. For example, arriving at work to find the copy machine broken may elicit a string of negative thoughts: *Now I won't be able to give the quiz as planned. We will get behind on the curriculum map. Students will then do poorly on the end of course exam.* Instead, pause and view the situation as objectively as possible: *The copy machine is broken.* Then, ponder how to respond to the problem in terms of improvement. Instead of the negatives, how can you leverage the problem for current or future benefit? *The copy machine is broken. This will give us one more day to review the more difficult parts of the content. The copy machine is broken. Now students can take the quiz in the computer lab, which will more closely simulate the end of course exam.*

Persisting with a Problem

Finally, give yourself grace. It takes time to train your mind to pause a quick reaction, and instead, choose a helpful response. In the fast-paced classroom environment, we often feel pressured to deal with problems quickly, but this can exacerbate a challenge. Practice slowing down and focus on one step at a time. With practice, you'll become more adept at handling problems in a way that leads to better outcomes for your students and less stress for you.

 ## Questions for Reflection

Think of a recent challenge you encountered in your classroom.
What was your initial reaction to the challenge?
What story did you tell yourself about the situation?
Was your story helpful?
Looking at the situation objectively, can you identify opportunities for potential improvement within the challenge?
How might regularly looking for the opportunities hidden in problems increase your impact and your satisfaction in teaching?

Notes and Works Cited

Gladwell, M. (2019). *Talking to strangers: What we should know about the people we don't know* (1st ed.). Little, Brown and Company.

Hasson, J. S. (2022). *Safe, seen, and stretched in the classroom: The remarkable ways teachers shape students' lives.* Routledge.

Gottman, J. M. (2011). *The science of trust: Emotional attunement for couples* (1st ed.). W. W. Norton.

Noddings, N. (1992). *The challenge to care in schools: An alternative approach to education.* Teachers College Press.

Shapiro, S. L. (2020). *Good morning, I love you: Mindfulness and self-compassion practices to rewire your brain for calm, clarity and joy.* Sounds True.

Hughes, J., Jacobson, T., Broderick, M., Ruck, A., Sara, M., Jones, J., Grey, J., … Paramount Pictures Corporation. (1987). *Ferris Bueller's day off.* Paramount Pictures Corp.

2

The Power of Pondering

The fog was thick in the valley but began to lift as I headed east toward Briarwood Elementary School. About ten miles en route, my thoughts began to drift to the countless items on my to-do list, but I was pulled back into the present moment by an incoming call. I pushed the button to accept and heard Cailin's voice over the speaker. My daughter, Cailin, was preparing to teach her third graders that morning. "I'm just not feeling it today," she confided. She sounded tired and discouraged, not the norm for this passionate third year teacher. She explained the directives her team had received from the district reading department the day before. "We've been told that students must always be reading books on their assigned level during choice reading time, and we must formally assess their comprehension on every book. We are also supposed to limit read aloud time and have a formal assessment for that, too. I feel like the magic of reading is being lost for them, and the magic of teaching reading is slowly fading away for me."

I just listened and tried not to give advice, a difficult move for this mom and former principal turned professor. Like many other teachers, Cailin thrives when she is able to be creative in her classroom. Limiting her autonomy and creativity was draining her energy. I wondered if it was also limiting her ability to be responsive to her students' needs and make an impact. It seems limiting options in instruction might also limit decisions around how to respond to students when challenges arise. Could

DOI: 10.4324/9781003344735-3

overly prescriptive directives work against a teacher's ability to turn problems into opportunities in the classroom? At the very least, limiting teachers' autonomy undermines their confidence in their own ability to respond to challenges.

I was certain Sara Stein Greenburg, the Executive Director of the Stanford Institute of design (and a creativity researcher) would caution school and district administrators against directives that limit creativity. According to Dr. Greenburg, it's quite unlikely that we will come up with an innovative way to meet a need if we've already been given a prescribed step. It's through open-ended questions, exploring, and experimenting that we find the best approach. We must also become comfortable with ambiguity, take time to sit with a problem, and consider multiple pathways in order to find the best solution. The most impactful teachers are constantly seeking information and trying different strategies. Cailin's call helped me understand that limiting teachers' choices limits their options for reaching a student, for igniting a spark, and for staying engaged in their work. I thought about the relationship between creativity and impact until I turned into the entrance to Briarwood Elementary.

Leading with Questions

I arrived just as the last of the buses was unloading, and I watched the principal, Sarah Ross, greet the students as they rushed inside. When the last student was safely in class, we headed into the main building where Sarah poured two mugs of coffee before walking me to her office. Sarah had been the principal of Briarwood for 18 months, with me as her principal coach. I noticed her confidence growing through each of our monthly coaching visits. While we were catching up over coffee, I told her I'd been wondering about the power of pausing for teachers. Could pausing before responding help them leverage moments of potential impact? She thought for a second before suggesting that pausing might be a powerful practice for principals, too. Then she shared a memory about Mrs. Keely, her principal when she was a new second grade teacher.

"I was so anxious about my first observation. I remember not sleeping at all the night before," Sarah began. "When the bell rang at the start of that day, I noticed Kenny (the student who challenged me most) wasn't there. I thought that might be a good thing since his behavior was sometimes unpredictable and disruptive." Sarah admitted feeling disappointed when the guidance counselor escorted Kenny into the classroom after the school day had begun. She could tell he was not having a good morning. "The counselor told me police had come to the door of Kenny's home during the night and arrested his father." Sarah took a sip of her coffee. "I got the other students started on their work and sat at a table in the back with Kenny. I asked him if he wanted to talk about it, but he just shook his head. I gave him some space at the back table for a bit and told him he could join the class when he felt ready."

When the time came for Mrs. Keely to observe Sarah's class, Kenny was still at the back table, but he was settled and quiet.

"I didn't know what to do, so I just let him stay there," she continued. "But during the observation, he started yelling out answers and making noises. He seemed to want attention, but he refused to leave the table and join the class. I watched Mrs. Keely taking notes and was sure she must have thought I was a terrible teacher."

When Mrs. Keely finished, she left a note on Sarah's desk before walking out the door. Sarah ran over to read it, certain it would say she needed more classroom management training. Instead, the note said, *Students like Kenny are puzzles sometimes. Let's brainstorm some ideas together.* Sarah realized her principal wasn't judging; she was wondering. "We had countless talks about Kenny," Sarah explained, "which always started with Mrs. Keely asking questions. She modeled the importance of pausing, pushing aside assumptions, and coming from a place of curiosity." Sarah described Mrs. Keely as her model of an effective principal. After hearing her story, I could see Mrs. Keely's influence on Sarah's leadership, her penchant for asking questions and commitment to her teachers' growth.

Humble Inquiry

Like Mrs. Keely, authors Edgar and Peter Shein advocate for leadership based on humble inquiry, the art of asking questions with genuine curiosity and interest in the other person. It's a commitment to acknowledging what we don't know and our need for information from others. Telling, unlike inquiring, is built on assumptions and arrogance. When we tell instead of ask, we imply that we know more and that our knowledge is more correct or valid. When we humbly ask and deeply listen, we acknowledge the wisdom of others. A principal cannot possibly know the needs of the students or the challenges in a particular classroom as well as the teacher. And so, principals need to elicit information from teachers in order to lead effectively. But information is only shared openly in cultures built on trust. Principals are wise to spend time building trust because people withhold information when it doesn't feel safe to speak the truth. And principals need open, honest communication to make good decisions. After all, decisions are only as good as the information on which they are based.

Humble inquiry is a necessary practice for teachers as well. Making decisions based on assumptions about students' needs is unreliable. The most effective instruction and classroom management decisions are based on accurate information obtained directly from students. We need to know what our students know in order to teach them. But students will be reluctant to reveal needs, ideas, and feedback until they trust us. Students are also more likely to share information when they feel valued and believe the information they share will be used. Asking with an open mind, deeply listening, and being responsive are necessary actions for getting the information we need. As teachers and leaders, admitting what we don't know requires humility and vulnerability, but our willingness to practice humble inquiry deepens relationships and increases our impact.

Wondering out Loud

After we finished our conversation, Sarah invited me to shadow her during classroom walkthroughs. She carried a clipboard on which she would jot down her questions and later use them to facilitate conversations with teachers. I knew that Sarah often went back to classrooms after school so that she could follow up with teachers when students were gone. These quiet moments gave them the space to talk openly and share their needs. I noted how comfortable teachers seemed with Sarah in the room. They were used to her visits, and she had intentionally built trust with each one of them. Just as we left the third classroom, Sarah got an urgent message on the radio. She was needed in room 211 immediately.

By the time we got to the doorway of 211, the teacher next door had already taken all of the children into her classroom—except for one. A small curly haired boy was lying face down on the carpet. His teacher, Naomi Jenkins, was kneeling next to him. Papers and books were strewn across the floor and chairs had been knocked over. In the middle of the mess, Naomi softly and silently rubbed the boy's back until his breathing slowed and his body relaxed. The guidance counselor arrived and persuaded him to walk with her. Sarah asked Naomi if she needed a break, but the young teacher wanted to get back to teaching. We helped her pick up the items on the floor, and she went next door to retrieve her students.

As we walked back toward the office, Sarah told me about Thomas. His outbursts were happening more frequently. They seemed to come out of nowhere and escalate quickly. The counselor had been working with him and trying different interventions; so Thomas stayed with her for the rest of that morning and returned to his class after lunch. Sarah and I walked by room 211 to check on Naomi twice that afternoon, but all was well. For such a young teacher, Naomi seemed remarkably unshaken. I wondered if her trust in Sarah had helped her feel more confident in the face of this challenge.

After the students were all dismissed and headed home for the day, Sarah and I found Naomi waiting in the office. I expected her to cry in frustration, vent about Thomas' behavior, or ask that he be moved to another class. She would have been justified in any of those responses. Instead, Naomi wondered out loud, "I wonder why it's so difficult for Thomas to cope with frustration? I wonder what he is thinking when these outbursts begin?" Sarah listened carefully and validated Naomi's concerns. She assured the young teacher that they would come up with a plan, and she reassured her that everyone would continue working together to support Thomas. Then she asked Naomi about her own well-being and inquired about her needs. True to her practice, Sarah withheld any judgment and resisted the urge to dispense advice.

Understanding the Why

As I drove back up the mountain toward Boone, I thought about Naomi and Thomas and how puzzling student behavior can be. As teachers, we see the outward manifestation, but it's difficult to know what's happening on the inside. In order to effectively deal with challenging behavior, we have to get a glimpse of the inner workings, we have to ask questions. Jessica Minahan (an educator) and Nancy Rappaport (a psychiatrist) teamed up to write *The Behavior Code: A Practical Guide to Understanding and Teaching the Most Challenging Students*, providing guidance for teachers dealing with difficult student behavior. They assert that in order to be effective, teachers must first understand what drives a student's behavior. Once the reason for the behavior is understood, we can implement strategies to help the student. For example, if a student is struggling to get along with peers, the underlying issue may be a lack of perspective-taking or the ability to share. Minahan and Rappaport prescribe a process that includes generating hypotheses, looking for patterns, and trying out accommodations.

According to these authors, students with challenging behaviors are more likely to succeed in classrooms where teachers are patient and open-minded. In the midst of a busy school day, behaviors are often dealt with expediently. The teacher comes to a quick conclusion about why a student acted inappropriately and provides a consequence based on that conclusion. A quick verbal correction or redirection works for most students most of the time. However, the behavior of the most challenging students often doesn't fit the usual patterns. It can be confusing, and the intent of the behavior may be difficult to recognize. Making an incorrect assumption can lead to an ineffective response, or worse, a response that exacerbates the behavior. Pausing to more accurately interpret the behavior and understand the motivation can make all the difference.

The Power of Pondering

Pulling into the parking lot at Appalachian State, I thought about Sarah and Naomi, and their penchant for pausing. Sarah always paused before responding to her teachers. Naomi paused before responding to Thomas. But it seemed there was more to their effectiveness than a pause alone. Both of these educators also made a habit of asking questions in order to help them learn valuable information about the people they were serving. In asking, they communicated to others that they matter, that their input has value. By posing questions, they established an environment where curiosity and reflection are important parts of the work.

Feeling judged, or even misunderstood, can damage a relationship. No one likes incorrect assumptions about their actions or intentions. It's easy to quickly create a narrative or fill in the blanks of someone else's story. Seeking to understand the experiences of another through genuine curiosity and care takes more time, but it pays off in deeper trust and stronger relationships. Everyone longs to feel known and understood, which only happens when we suspend judgment and listen with the purpose of finding the answer to the question, *What's it like to be you?*

Questions are essential to strong relationships, and they are also a path to our own growth. They can keep us from feeling stagnant and stuck, but in some instances, asking questions can also be uncomfortable. Certainty makes us feel like we're in control, but wandering into uncertainty can feel a bit unsettling. Embracing uncertainty has its rewards though. Pausing and pondering can lead us to new ideas and insights. We can begin to see possible solutions to problems that once seemed insurmountable and begin to understand the experiences of others. Instead of rushing to answers, lingering longer and asking questions is a beneficial practice for teachers and leaders.

Wondering about Learning

I made it back to my office on campus just in time for my meeting with Austin, an English Education major working through an assignment to interview a professor about research. Talking with undergraduate students who are preparing to teach always gives me hope. I love their excitement, even if they are a bit idealistic. Austin came rushing in, pulled off his jacket, and sat in the blue pleather chair across from my desk. We chatted about his classes, and he asked me the questions required for his project. Then I asked Austin why he chose teaching as his future career.

"I guess it was Mr. Brady, my chemistry teacher, who inspired me," he said, pushing his laptop back into his backpack. "I hate to admit that I was failing chemistry. I hadn't done well on the first two tests, and I stopped to talk with my teacher after school. I asked Mr. Brady for suggestions, and I still remember him saying that he was the expert on chemistry, but I was the expert on me, and we would figure it out together."

Austin recalled his teacher asking him to describe the times when he felt like he was learning and the times when he felt like he was struggling in class. "I told him I learned best in labs when I could talk about the concepts with my lab partner and that I felt overwhelmed when he was doing demonstrations. Watching and listening while taking notes at the same time was too much for me."

Mr. Brady and Austin did come up with some ideas. Austin would schedule study dates with his lab partner so they could work together on the review pages. He would also watch a series of videos Mr. Brady recommended. With videos, he could pause to take notes and go back to rewatch segments as needed. "I had never really reflected on how I learn best before. Mr. Brady's questions prompted me to consider what I needed as a learner. I really appreciate how much Mr. Brady cared about me. It's something I want to carry into my own teaching, helping my students understand how they learn." Austin turned back to tell me one more thing before heading out the door: "By the way, I ended up with a B in Chemistry."

Care, Curiosity, and Connection

Researchers Kristy Cooper and Andrew Miness investigated the co-creation of caring in student-teacher relationships. They interviewed students about their relationships with teachers and found students expected to see caring as a virtue in their teachers. In other words, teachers who expressed caring about students collectively from in front of the classroom met students' expectations, but they weren't perceived as exceptionally caring. Teachers who were relationally caring, who engaged in one-on-one interactions in which they expressed a personal interest in students were described as exceeding expectations. These teachers made an impact on students' academic, social, and emotional experiences in school.

The researchers also found that understanding is a necessary component of relational caring. The most effective teachers seek to understand the perspectives and needs of individual students in order to demonstrate relational care. Students feel most cared for when they perceive their teachers understand them as learners and as people, just as Mr. Brady did for Austin. Strong relationships are not an accident; they are the product of consistent choices. When an event happens in the classroom, teachers must intentionally make choices that demonstrate care in order to build relationships. With all of the daily demands on teachers, this isn't easy.

However, a teacher's effort alone isn't enough to forge a strong relationship. Relationships are co-created, and students get to decide how much information to share. The willingness of individual students to disclose needs and personal information depends upon each student's feelings of comfort and safety in the relationship. Some students are more cautious, but even with the most guarded students, teachers can demonstrate understanding of the challenges around the age and life stage of the student in general. Just trying to connect and understand sends a message of care and valuing. Growth requires engagement on the part of the student, and students are much more likely to engage with teachers who care about their lives inside and outside of the classroom. It's important to understand *who* our students are and *how* they are before we get to the business of teaching them.

Pausing and Pondering

Before packing up and heading home, I pulled out my journal to jot down some thoughts. I'd made an effort to slow down and be more attentive and open minded throughout the day. When I was tempted to talk more than listen in my conversations with Cailin, Sarah, and Austin, I paused. I could see how the practice of pausing could build stronger connections. Witnessing the power of pausing in Naomi's response to Thomas inspired me. The pause allowed her to choose a caring response rather than give in to emotions in the moment. I could see how pausing prevented an unhelpful response, but it takes more than pausing to create a positive impact.

Pausing was the start, but pondering was the crucial next step. First pausing then pondering allows educators to generate possible options. Pausing then suspending judgment and assumptions in favor of genuine curiosity allows us to focus our attention and seek understanding. I could see how the effort to slow down and try to understand students' experiences and perspectives would help students feel seen and valued. I could also see how the information gleaned from asking questions and deeply listening would help teachers arrive at better solutions to problems in the classroom. It seemed simple, just pausing and pondering, but in a noisy and hectic world, it isn't easy.

"Be curious, not judgmental," is a quote often attributed to Walt Whitman, but scholars disagree about this attribution. The quote experienced a recent revival when Ted Lasso, a perennially positive television character, used it in a monologue. Regardless of the quote's origin, it's a good advice. Be curious, wonder, listen, welcome the unknown. Resist the urge to judge and avoid hasty assumptions. When we are genuinely curious, we are more thoughtful and make more intentional decisions. We are less likely to act in haste and create additional problems for ourselves and others. When we are open minded about others' perspectives, we strengthen relationships. Practicing curiosity over judgment can be a path to less regret and greater impact. I thought about Cailin's call earlier that morning. Would district leaders have served students better if they had engaged teachers in conversations about their young readers' needs? Surely, coming from a stance of curiosity rather than certainty could have revealed helpful information for everyone involved.

Driven by my own sense of wonder, I wanted to find more examples of pausing and pondering in practice. I was heading to Southside High School in Florida next week, and I knew I would find more opportunities to witness curiosity over judgment on my trip. I'd worked with the leadership team and faculty at Southside a few years ago and was eager to check on their progress. They had been intentionally focused on building a collaborative culture. A culture steeped in collaboration and innovation would surely offer insight into transforming problems into opportunities.

Leveraging the Power of a Problem

Pausing with Curiosity

Cultivating genuine curiosity is a necessary practice in turning problems into opportunities. When faced with a challenge, pause for a moment to give yourself time to push aside your own initial emotions and assume an open-minded stance toward the challenge. Slow down to give yourself time to reframe the challenge as an opportunity, gather helpful information, and generate the best possible options.

Pondering with Curiosity

Pondering entails asking questions from a place of genuine care and interest. This type of questioning requires both humility and vulnerability as it infers the other person knows something you need to know in order to be effective. Open-ended questions are most helpful: *Can you help me understand____? What part of _____ is most difficult for you? How could I best support you in ____?*

Once a question is posed, listen with the intent to understand. Focus attentively on what the other person is saying, and try to understand the feelings and perspectives behind the words. Push aside your own perspectives and biases. Avoid becoming distracted by your own thoughts or need to respond.

Persisting with Curiosity

Be willing to wrestle with uncertainty, even when it feels uncomfortable. Be willing to admit what you don't yet know. By acknowledging that there is a bigger picture and you can only see part of it from your position, you can acquire the information you need to find the best solution. Engaging those you serve with care and curiosity can lead you to potential improvements you could not have identified on your own. You may have to seek more information, revisit and adjust your plans as you move forward, but just keep moving forward.

Questions for Reflection

Think about the information you need to help students achieve better academic, social, and emotional outcomes. How can you engage students in sharing information that could help you help them?

How can you integrate this type of inquiry regularly into your practice?

How can you build trusting relationships that will make students more likely to share information with you?

How might regularly practicing curiosity and care increase your impact and your satisfaction in teaching?

Notes and Works Cited

Stein Greenberg, S. (2021). *Creative acts for curious people: How to think, create, and lead in unconventional ways.* Ten Speed.

Schein, E. H. (2013). *Humble inquiry: The gentle art of asking instead of telling.* Berrett-Koehler Publishers, Inc.

Cooper, K. S. & Miness, A. (2014). The co-creation of caring student-teacher relationships: Does teacher understanding matter? *The High School Journal, 97*(4), 264–290.

Minahan, J. & Rappaport, N. (2020). *The behavior code: A practical guide to understanding and teaching the most challenging students.* Harvard Education Press.

Harmsen, R., Helms-Lorenz, M., Maulana, R., & Van Veen, K. (2018). The relationship between beginning teachers' stress causes, stress responses, teaching behaviour and attrition. *Teachers and Teaching: Theory and Practice, 24*(6), 626–643.

Lawrence, B., Sudeikis, J., Hunt, B., Kelly, J., Ingold, J., & Wrubel, B. (2020). *Ted Lasso: Season 1 Episode 8.* Apple TV.

3

The Power of Persisting

It took ten hours to drive from North Carolina to Central Florida. I arrived just as the sun was going down and just in time to meet my friend, Laura, at our favorite barbeque restaurant. I stepped out of the car and into the parking lot, which was still steamy after a late afternoon rainstorm. The warm air felt like a familiar embrace from my home state. I found Laura at a table in the corner, having already ordered iced tea and fried pickles. After four decades of friendship, it takes little time to catch up and jump right into a conversation. Scooping a spoonful of pickles onto her plate, Laura asked, "What've you been working on?"

"I'm digging into a phenomenon I've noticed in the data," I explained as I placed a checkered napkin on my lap. "In many of the stories, when a difficult situation happens in a classroom, a teacher finds a way to use that situation to make a positive impact." I told my friend about Marcus taking the cookies, Danielle falling asleep, and Austin failing the test. I told her about the ways their teachers withheld reactions and assumptions, and instead, asked questions and offered support.

Laura agreed that teaching is fraught with tests of patience, but it's also loaded with opportunities for impact. We talked about the decision point between a student's actions and a teacher's response. In that moment, our choices can help or harm. After over two decades as an English teacher (most of it spent teaching advanced placement literature), Laura had recently become the lead teacher for English Language Learners at her

DOI: 10.4324/9781003344735-4

school, and this new role brought new challenges. I asked my friend if she could share an example of turning a problem into an opportunity in her own classroom.

"I try to reduce the anxiety and increase the fun in learning. I want my students to develop the confidence to speak in English," Laura began, passing me the ranch dressing for dipping. "The students enjoy reader's theater, and it's become a regular instructional strategy for us. I let them choose the parts they'll read the day before we perform the play so they can practice. We've got the structure down, so I was surprised when we hit a bump a few weeks ago."

Laura explained that on that particular day, students began reading but the flow stopped abruptly when Marisol's part came up. She described the way Marisol just sat there, frozen, refusing to read. "At first I felt frustrated," Laura admitted. "But I wanted to keep the others engaged, so I just asked one of my stronger students to take Marisol's part."

Laura asked Marisol to stay and talk with her after class. Suddenly, the silent student could hardly get the words out fast enough. Marisol shared the news that her mother was not doing well back in Mexico. She wasn't sure exactly what was wrong or the severity of the issue, but she was overcome with worry. She also confessed her fear that she would have to return to her home country to help her mother. She believed that if she returned, she would never make it back to the United States.

"There was nothing I could do to improve the situation for her," Laura explained. "I just listened, and listening helped. As Marisol talked, her tension seemed to lessen."

Laura and I acknowledged the importance of listening and trying to understand. Teachers spend much of their time talking, but listening can be equally powerful. For Laura's students, her willingness to listen not only demonstrated care, it also provided authentic opportunities for them to communicate relevant information in English. My friend understood the importance of building her students' confidence. Her students had high efficacy (belief in their ability to influence an outcome) in many contexts, but not necessarily in the classroom. Many of her students had navigated difficult life situations.

They certainly saw themselves as survivors, but did they see themselves as learners?

Academic Self-Efficacy

Researcher Jim Soland has studied the role self-efficacy plays in the achievement of students like Laura's. These students have the challenge of learning a new language while continuing to build academic skills in core subjects. In addition to not yet being proficient in English, many have limited or interrupted school experiences. Older students in particular may have missed schooling in their home countries due to civil unrest, migration, or the unavailability of schools. The lack of native language literacy and other academic skills make it difficult for older students to catch up with their grade-level peers. English Language Learners tend to perform below grade level in every subject, and Dr. Soland has found a relationship between academic performance and academic self-efficacy.

Academic self-efficacy is a student's confidence in the ability to attain educational goals. It is a building block for motivation, achievement, and persistence. If students don't believe in their ability to accomplish challenging tasks, they are unlikely to attempt them. They are also unlikely to persist through difficulty. With the obstacles and barriers English Language Learners must overcome, self-efficacy is critical. With low academic self-efficacy related to slower growth in reading and math, these students need to build efficacy in order to catch up with their peers.

Laura's attention to the social and emotional needs of her students was a step in the right direction. A positive mood can increase self-efficacy, while anxiety can undermine it. Reducing stressful situations and lowering anxiety surrounding events like exams or presentations contributes to greater success. Engaging students while maintaining a culture safe for taking learning risks is a way to help students develop confidence. Collaborative projects have the dual outcome of improving both self-efficacy and social skills. When students work together and help one another, they tend to appraise their own capability more highly. I praised my friend for her effective pedagogy and for her commitment to her students. She had provided a safe space for students as she carefully scaffolded their learning. And her demonstrations of care helped each student feel seen.

I appreciated Laura's story and her candor about her initial feelings of frustration in the moment with Marisol. Her inclination to suspend an emotional reaction, willingness to inquire about Marisol's situation, and effort to continue providing support was a useful example for me. I agreed to keep my friend posted on my progress, and after finishing our meal, we walked back out to the parking lot together.

Southside High School

After a decent night of sleep in a hotel bed, I headed to Southside High School to lead their professional development day. The driveway to Southside is lined with tall palm trees leading to a cluster of beige buildings connected by outside hallways. I found a spot near the front and walked down a covered walkway to the office. I pressed the buzzer outside the door, and Melanie Byrd, the administrative assistant, let me in. We chatted as she walked me to the back of the office and handed me off to Ben Johnson, the principal. Ben (as usual) was wearing a suit and a pair of Converse tennis shoes. He is tall to begin with, but his energetic presence makes him seem even bigger.

Once in his office, we went over the plan for the day. I'd provided professional development to the Southside faculty before, but the pandemic prompted Ben to bring me back. During our planning conversations, Ben expressed concerns that pandemic challenges had lessened his teachers' resolve. "I think the physical and mental exhaustion has done a number on their confidence," he said. "I used to consider us a thriving team, but now I think we are just surviving." When we created the agenda, we decided to focus on resilience, the ability to withstand adversity and bounce back from difficult events. Being resilient does not mean freedom from stress and suffering, but rather, having the ability to process and overcome hardship. Educators with low resilience may get easily overwhelmed and feel stuck when challenges come. Luckily, resilience is a dynamic trait which can be developed and strengthened over time.

I also shared the relationship between resilience and efficacy with Ben. Psychologists Albert Bandura and Charles Benight found that confidence in one's ability to cope with traumatic events aids in recovery from different types of traumatic experiences. In other words, strong belief in our ability to manage the events that affect our lives limits the negative impact of stressful or traumatic events. When we believe we have some control over difficult situations, we are less likely to perceive those situations as catastrophic. If we believe our own actions have the power to produce better circumstances, we are more likely to take the steps needed to improve our lives. Since our levels of efficacy are impacted by our physical and mental states, exhaustion certainly lessens efficacy and—because they are connected—reduces resilience. This has certainly been true for educators navigating challenges related to the pandemic.

After talking through the needs of his faculty and deciding to focus on resilience, Ben and I homed in on three ways we could develop the concept. First, I would provide stories of teachers who persevered through challenges to impact students' lives. These stories would allow teachers to experience success vicariously through the stories, and vicarious experiences are one way to increase efficacy. Next, Ben would share stories of his teacher's own past successes. Recalling their own experiences of mastery would also help bolster their sense of efficacy. Finally, we would give teachers time to discuss the potential goals they might consider next. Giving teachers a voice in decision-making would help them feel a greater sense of control over their work. There was much in Southside's existing culture to build upon. They just needed to be reminded of their successes and encouraged to continue leaning on each other.

Thriving Teams

Ben and I made our way to the auditorium and found Jackie Crawford, a math teacher, at the coffee bar outside. I stopped to grab a tea while Ben went in to check the sound system. As I dunked a tea bag in my cup of hot water, I asked Jackie how she was doing. "I'm not going to lie—it's been a tough year," she said. "I kept thinking this year would be easier now that we are all back on campus, but it just feels hard and heavy."

I asked her if she'd found any helpful strategies for dealing with the challenges. "The kids really do keep me going," she confessed. "And the stories you email each week always give me a lift." I was thrilled that she found my weekly emails helpful. I'd tried to provide the teachers on my email list with a weekly dose of inspiration, especially during the pandemic. "Speaking of stories," Jackie added, "I've been thinking I need to tell you about Miss Machin, my high school math teacher." We still had a few minutes before the session was to begin, so I invited her to share the story with me.

"I've always loved math, and I've always been pretty good at it," Jackie began, tearing open a packet of sweetener and dumping it into her coffee. "I was in Miss Machin's trigonometry class my junior year, along with four of my friends. We were the only girls in the class, and Miss Machin called us The Fab Five. When the spring math competitions were approaching, our teacher asked us if we wanted to compete as a team."

Jackie described the hours they spent practicing and preparing, motivated by Miss Machin's enthusiasm. "She had so much belief in us that we started to believe in ourselves. I wasn't confident that I could solve all the problems, but I was confident that together we could figure anything out." Jackie revealed that the team did win most of their competitions. "I loved being on that team, and my colleagues in the math department here remind me a bit of those days. We work together to solve problems. We share resources, and we really encourage each other."

Jackie and I agreed that Miss Machin was a model for building collective efficacy, a team's shared belief that through their unified efforts they can overcome challenges and produce intended results. Because Jackie's team developed a strong belief in their collective ability, they experienced greater success. I thought Jackie's memory of Miss Machin would be a perfect addition to our session, and she agreed to share her story with the faculty later in the morning. With a story in our hearts and hot drinks in our hands, we headed into the auditorium to prepare.

Collective Teacher Efficacy

Our professional development session began with me sharing inspirational stories as examples of teachers turning challenges into opportunities for impact. We then dug more deeply into each story to pull out useful strategies that this group of tired teachers could easily implement. We talked about the habit of pausing and taking a breath before responding, and they could see how this mindful habit might increase their sense of peace and resilience. The benefit of a curious stance also seemed to speak to this groups' reflective nature. It was important they didn't see the practices of pausing and pondering as just another initiative or something else to add to their plates. Instead, it was a shift in mindset. It required awareness, commitment, and willingness to move together toward more impactful practices for students and more satisfaction for themselves.

During our session, Ben and his leadership team shared stories of their teachers' past successes and the countless students whose lives they had impacted. The leaders gave example after example of how their teachers had overcome barriers to help their students succeed. I could almost feel hope return, and the teachers seemed to sit up a bit taller. They remembered that they know how to deal with challenges in the classroom. We then talked about potential new goals and put teachers into small groups to come to consensus on which ones were achievable considering the current situation. Giving them a voice in decision-making helped them feel empowered, and putting them in teams helped to instill a sense of collective efficacy.

Researcher Jenni Donohoo defines collective teacher efficacy as a shared belief that teachers have the ability to influence student outcomes. When teachers believe that they can make a difference, they are more likely to take on a challenge and persist in that challenge. When they believe they can reach their goals, they are more likely to pursue those goals. Efficacy beliefs help determine where teachers focus their efforts and how much effort they are willing to expend. And since much of the work in schools is interdependent, collective efficacy beliefs are essential for impacting student outcomes. Dr. Donohoo identified building cohesive teams, giving teachers autonomy, and providing structures for shared decision-making as leader behaviors that help increase collective teacher efficacy.

Ben had integrated these actions into our professional development session, and his teachers responded with renewed confidence. When Jackie shared her story about Miss Machin, she provided her colleagues with a beautiful model of collective efficacy. And through Ben's stories of their own successes, they remembered their strength. The way Ben communicated belief in his teachers' collective ability helped them believe in the power of their team. We wrapped up the session on a high note, and everyone headed down to the cafeteria for lunch.

Design Thinking

After lunch, I walked through classrooms with Ben to check in with teachers and answer any questions. In one of the rooms, we found a team of teachers working with the guidance counselor and social worker on a persistent issue. They had a list of students who were frequently absent, and together, they decided to find a way to improve the students' attendance. The counselor explained that they were using design thinking to analyze the problem and create a plan. At this point, they were still in the information-gathering phase, considering the unique circumstances and barriers for each student. They had talked with both students and parents, using an empathetic and genuinely curious approach to gain the information they needed. The group of problem-solvers was preparing to identify some potential root causes of the problem and generate ideas for addressing those causes. Once they drafted their plan, they would collect data in order to evaluate and tweak the plan as needed.

Like this group of educators, professor and author Andrew Pressman is an advocate for using design thinking to approach problems. Dr. Pressman describes design thinking as a creative and dynamic process with no hard and fast rules. Rather, it is a mindset for generating fresh perspectives and new solutions. Design thinkers embrace ambiguity and acknowledge what is unknown. They follow their instincts and generate ideas without judgment. They also acknowledge the essential role of failure. After all, bad ideas can be a launching point for exceptional solutions. Most importantly, design thinkers view constraints as opportunities. They know that obstacles force teams to get creative. I had to acknowledge the ways pausing and pondering were integral parts of design thinking. And this team provided a beautiful model of collective efficacy.

From Plan to Action

Just as I was about to leave, one of the teachers, Amber Neil, asked if she could share a story about her high school teacher. Our morning professional development session had her thinking about Mr. Frye. The group (ready for a break) encouraged her to share.

"I took a programming class in high school because I was interested in computers," Amber began. "I wanted to understand how programs work. But I didn't anticipate that programming was much more about doing than passively understanding." Amber described how her perfectionist tendencies and penchant for overthinking sometimes made taking action a challenge. Amber's colleagues nodded, recognizing and understanding her reason for sometimes feeling stuck.

"One day, Mr. Frye kept me after class to talk. He suggested I might be trying to avoid failure by forever staying in the planning phase. After all, there's no risk in planning. Mr. Frye convinced me that no plan is foolproof, even the most carefully crafted. He told me the best programs often come from trial and error. He encouraged me to put down the plan and take a first step".

Amber credited Mr. Frye with forever changing the way she looked at failure. "I began to see my mistakes as paths to improvement. I learned to stop getting paralyzed in the planning and take action, knowing I could make adjustments and try again. Mr. Frye not only helped me learn about programming, he helped me learn about courage. When I find myself overthinking, I still hear his voice encouraging me to "just give it a go.""

Grateful for Amber's story, we all marveled at the genius of Mr. Frye. Planning is important, but only if the plan is tested. Improvement only comes with trying and tweaking. Amber's colleagues vowed to keep this in mind as they moved forward in their effort to improve the student attendance problem. I felt lucky to have been a witness to this group's collaboration. They had given me much to consider about turning challenges into opportunities for impact. It was a perfect way to end my day at Southside.

Persisting

My drive back to North Carolina provided plenty of time for reflecting. I thought about Laura's efforts to support her English Language Learners. I considered the lessons Jackie carried from her year with Miss Machin. I contemplated the ways Ben supported the efficacy of his teachers, and I recounted my discussion with the team using design thinking to improve student attendance. Certainly, all of them practiced pausing and pondering. Being mindful and curious was evident in the work of all these educators. But there was something else going on. They all demonstrated a commitment to keep trying, even when making an impact on students was difficult. They were committed to staying the course, even when they had to adjust their steps. In other words, they persisted.

Regular planning is critical for teaching and leading, but persistence may be even more important. In classrooms and schools, things don't usually go as planned. The most impactful educators are ready when the inevitable challenges get in the way. They understand that problems are an unavoidable part of the work, and they keep going. Great teachers and leaders experience failures and learn from them. There are always unexpected barriers and things out of our control, but those are the very moments we have the potential to make an impact.

My thoughts sometimes wander to random places on a long drive, and thinking about persisting made me think of the novel *The Martian* by Andy Weir. In the book (and the movie it inspired starring Matt Damon), astronaut Mark Watney finds himself stranded on Mars after the rest of the crew presumes him dead and leaves him behind. He has no way to get a signal to Earth, and he would certainly run out of supplies before anyone could rescue him. But Mark refuses to give up. Drawing on his ingenuity, engineering skills, and incredible persistence, he works through challenge after challenge. Mark finds a way to cultivate food, and he fashions the tools he needs from scavenged parts of previous missions. Instead of panicking, he pauses. He keeps an open mind, and he ponders his way to creative solutions. He persists through an unbelievable maze of seemingly insurmountable obstacles. This fictional character's process looks much like the steps educators take to turn problems into opportunities for impact in classrooms and schools.

Pausing and pondering are the keys to an effective initial response, but persisting is necessary for reaching success. Pausing, pondering, and persisting are a promising framework for turning challenges into the opportunity to make an impact. And because making an impact gives purpose and meaning to our work, these practices could also be the path to finding a greater sense of satisfaction in teaching. The power of these practices was evident in many of the stories in my data, and I found multiple examples during my visits to schools. Now I wanted to talk with teachers about what I was finding. Would it resonate with them? I couldn't wait to hear their perspectives.

Leveraging the Power of Persisting

Persistent Pausing

Building your persistence muscle requires developing resilience. The first step is just taking a breath when you feel anxious. Deep breaths help you manage stress and anxiety in the moment but also long term. By consciously becoming aware of your breath and regulating its depth and rate, you can bring yourself back to a more calm and empowered state. When you feel yourself becoming anxious, place your hand on your abdomen. Breathe in while counting 1-2-3, hold while counting 4-5, and breathe out while counting 6-7-8. One of the best tools for managing stress is managing our own breathing.

Persistent Pondering

We all experience thinking traps. When a stressful situation occurs, it's human nature to fall into catastrophic thinking, expecting the worst possible outcome. It's best to stay in the present moment rather than projecting into an unknowable future. Instead, look at the situation objectively. Become aware of your thoughts. Ask, *What am I telling myself about this situation? What evidence do I have that this is true? What are other potential explanations?* Then choose the most empowering thoughts to help you move forward.

Consistent Persistence

Whenever a problem or challenge arises, remind yourself that you have the ability to navigate it. Consider the resources you have for dealing with the difficulty, especially supportive colleagues and friends. Your individual strength may be limited, but together you are exponentially stronger. A primary factor in resilience is having caring and supportive relationships within and outside the family. Take the time to cultivate relationships and lean on them when times get tough. Remember, nothing lasts forever. When hard times come, they will eventually pass.

Questions for Reflection

Think of a difficult situation you successfully navigated in the past.

What strategies helped you?

How could you apply these strategies to future challenges?

Who are the people in your life who provide support in difficult times?

What other resources help you deal with difficulty?

How can becoming more resilient help you become a more effective educator?

Notes and Works Cited

Soland, J., & Sandilos, L. E. (2021). English language learners, self-efficacy, and the achievement gap: Understanding the relationship between academic and social-emotional growth. *Journal of Education for Students Placed at Risk, 26*(1), 20–44.

Benight, C. C., & Bandura, A. (2004). Social cognitive theory of post-traumatic recovery: The role of perceived self-efficacy. *Behaviour Research and Therapy, 42*(10), 1129–1148.

Donohoo, J. (2017). *Collective efficacy: How educators' beliefs impact student learning.* Corwin.

Weir, A. (2014). *The Martian: A novel.* Random House, Inc., Crown Publishing.

4

The Power of Hope

If you walked into my office at Appalachian State University, you might assume I was an unusually organized professor. My desk and shelves are free from clutter, and all visible items are neatly displayed. But that assumption would quickly be proven false the minute you tried to open one of the drawers in my vertical file cabinet, my secret shame of hoarding copies of research articles revealed. This stash of stapled packets is not filed alphabetically or by topic. Rather, the articles are shoved into every file drawer in random piles until the drawers reach capacity and refuse to close. This system does not serve me well, and I often find myself digging through the piles in search of a particular article. Such was the case this morning as I searched for an article I promised to give a graduate student. Luckily, I came upon it fairly quickly and managed to close the drawer, but as I turned back to my desk, one article had fallen out and was lying on the floor. It was an article I added to my collection recently, written by Chan Hellman and his colleagues at the University of Oklahoma.

Dr. Hellman is the Founding Director of the Hope Research Center, which is focused on developing, testing, and implementing a trauma-informed and hope-centered framework for human service agencies. This particular article summarized his study of hope as a protective factor in lowering burnout among child welfare workers. Child welfare organizations have an unusually high turnover rate, negatively impacting the quality of care and

DOI: 10.4324/9781003344735-5

services provided to children and families. Large caseloads, lack of support, and constant exposure to children's suffering contribute to case worker burnout. Finding this particular article on the floor was a stroke of serendipity. I was heading to a focus group on teacher retention with six experienced educators. We planned to discuss reasons for the growing number of teachers leaving the profession, and I'd been wondering if those choosing to leave had lost hope.

According to Dr. Hellman, hope is the ability to envision a better future while taking goal-directed action toward that future in the face of adversity. Individuals with higher hope can identify multiple pathways to reach their goals. When an obstacle blocks one path, they move on to another option. Most people begin their careers in fields like child welfare or education with a high degree of hopefulness, but frequent frustration— caused by challenging working conditions, overload, and other impediments—can lead to emotional exhaustion and burnout. Those who maintain a high degree of hope are less likely to view problems as sources of stress, and instead, view them as an opportunity for growth and improvement. Therefore, higher hope is correlated with greater engagement and better performance. This does not mean that the responsibility for decreasing burnout and turnover falls squarely on the individual. Dr. Hellman suggests that organizations can support increased hope by helping employees identify goals and pathways to reach them while actively working to reduce obstacles and impediments. Identifying barriers, such as high caseloads and burdensome administrative demands are necessary tasks for child welfare organizations, and surely, removing barriers and lessening extraneous tasks could also benefit teachers. After reacquainting myself with the article, I was eager to meet with the focus group.

Talking Teacher Turnover

I walked down the hall and into our assigned classroom just as the first members of the focus group arrived. The six in this group were all women with more than a decade in teaching. After some greetings and small talk, we took our seats at a round table in the corner. I reminded the group that the topic of our discussion would be teacher retention and their responses would inform my understanding of the topic as well as my recommendations to school districts. With their shared experiences and passion for teaching, it was easy to get them started. I began by asking for their perspectives on why teachers were leaving the profession. Amy spoke first.

"It's become an impossible job," she said. "I think we all want to help students succeed, but there are so many stumbling blocks. It constantly feels like one step forward and two steps back."

When I asked the group to describe some of the barriers, Charisse chimed in. "It seems like the students' needs are getting greater and more intense," she said. "Many are struggling because they've experienced some type of trauma. It interferes with their academic success, and their behavior can be challenging. I just don't have the background or the skills to help them overcome it."

Shana validated her fellow teacher and added that additional counselors, social workers, and exceptional education teachers could provide the support that seemed beyond the capacity and time constraints of classroom teachers. The whole group nodded in agreement.

Wanting to explore Dr. Hellman's theory of hope as a protective factor against burnout, I asked them when they feel most hopeful in their professional lives. Unsurprisingly, they recounted moments of connection and success with students. But they also shared moments of connection and success with colleagues. Collaboratively pursuing a collective goal with the intention of impacting students was identified by this group of teachers as an activity that increases hope. Melissa shifted in her chair and offered an insight.

"When I'm working with a group of teachers who can see how something could be better and are willing to work together to figure it out and make it happen, I feel energized," she said.

"I hear you," Amy responded, "but the opposite is also true. When colleagues are negative and fatalistic, when they tell me change is impossible and things are never going to get better, it sucks the life out of me."

The discussion generated a whole list of hope-boosting and hope-draining situations. I inquired about what these experienced teachers do in hope-draining situations. Several members of the group named refocusing on their students and seeking supportive colleagues as workable strategies. Then Kasey wondered out loud if hope is really a noun or a verb. Her comment led to an epiphany: Maybe hope isn't something we have. Perhaps it's not something that can slip through our hands and be lost. What if hope is active and can be strengthened through practice? Our two-hour session flew by before we could dig deeply into actively practicing hope, but the focus group asked if we could meet again, and I enthusiastically agreed to schedule another session.

Hope as Action

The teachers headed out of the classroom, but Kasey stuck around. She said the discussion had been thought-provoking, and it brought back a memory about her fifth-grade teacher, Mrs. Collins. I asked Kasey if she would share the memory with me, and we both sat back down at the round table. Kasey explained that she lived with her mother and grandparents through most of her elementary school years. Her grandmother was the heart of their home and the one who held everything together, and when she died, the family was devastated. Kasey tucked her hair behind her ear.

"My mother and grandfather were so grief-stricken that they couldn't really talk with me and help me process the loss," she told me. "Luckily, Mrs. Collins knew the important role my grandmother played in my life, and she took the time to check on me."

Kasey shared the way her teacher would sit with her every morning to inquire about how she was doing. One morning, she told Mrs. Collins that she was worried about her mother and grandfather because they were so sad.

"I felt hopeless. I just wanted my family to be happy again," Kasey explained. "Mrs. Collins taught me a lesson I will never forget. She told me that hope is just imagining how we want things to be and figuring out how to make them so." Kasey said her teacher helped her come up with a list of things she could do to help her mother and grandfather. She drew pictures for them, helped cook meals, and convinced them to go for walks. "Each time I made my mother and grandfather smile, I felt a little more hopeful. I began to see how my efforts could make things better. It was a powerful lesson about the nature of hope."

Hope as a Practice

As I walked Kasey down the hall and to the elevator, I thought about her story and the way her teacher inspired her to take hopeful action. Patrick Shade, a professor of philosophy at Rhodes College, also sees hope as a practice rooted in our interactions within the context of our environment. He views hope through the pragmatic lens of philosophers, such as C. S. Peirce, William James, and John Dewey. Dr. Shade offers a theory of hope as realistic and productive, requiring both imagination and informed action. According to Dr. Shade, hope is strengthened through habits, which are defined in pragmatism as attitudes that are both emotional and intellectual. The habits provide the means by which we realize a hopeful end. They include resourcefulness, persistence, and courage. Resourcefulness helps us find ways to transcend our current limitations. The greater our resources, both material and internal, the more likely we are to reach the desired outcome. Persistence sustains us as we move along the path; it helps us develop the means to get to the end through consistency and commitment. Courage is necessary as we step into the change and growth required to see a dream realized and to risk the possibility of a dream deferred or denied.

Hoping from a pragmatic stance requires envisioning a better world while staying connected to the reality of the current one. Mrs. Collins took this stance with Kasey, acknowledging the heartbreak of her loss while holding out hope that joy would return one day. This is a useful outlook for educators, particularly those who work with students experiencing significant challenges. We can't simply wait for the world to change, choosing not to take action on the challenges our students are facing. Despite the obstacles, hope necessitates the identification of at least some stepping stones and resources that we can leverage to make things better. When we practice resourcefulness, we find ways to provide the things our students need. And we develop the resource most important for their success: our own skill in teaching. Through persistence, we make repeated efforts until we find what works. Through courage, we take risks and endure discomfort to walk with our students toward a brighter future. By practicing the habits of hope, we can see the goodness in our students, schools, and world, even through the challenges.

A Dream and a Plan

I had just enough time to grab a quick dinner before teaching my evening class. My colleague, Annie, passed me in the hallway and invited me to join her and some friends heading to Boone Saloon for a bite. I never turn down a chance for Saloon chili on a cool day, so Annie and I cut through the parking lot and headed up the steep wooden staircase to the entrance. We found our group at a high-top table, and I grabbed an open stool next to Matt, a faculty member in the political science department. We chatted about the day's happenings, and I shared how the topic of hope had captivated my focus group. Matt and I agreed teaching is a career that both employs hope and generates hope. He revealed that, in high school, one of his teachers helped him learn about hope and inspired him to pursue a career in political science. I was intrigued—to me, politics seemed like a field rich in cynicism and lacking in hope. I asked him to tell me more.

"I took a political science class my senior year of high school, mostly because I'd heard Mrs. Carter was a cool teacher," he began. Matt stirred the ice at the bottom of his soda with his straw. "She was so full of energy, and made me feel like I could do anything." He described a writing task Mrs. Carter assigned about halfway through the semester. She asked the class to address the prompt, *What kind of world do you want?* Students were to write about their vision of an ideal world, the kind they would want for future children. "That assignment was surprisingly difficult for me," Matt confessed. "I really had to tap into my values and think about my beliefs around individual rights, justice, and collective responsibility. I learned so much about my political views through that assignment."

We talked about the role of vision in hope. I shared highlights from Chan Hellman's work, the process of holding a vision, seeing a path, and persevering as a definition of hope. "That's interesting," Matt replied, "because later in the semester Mrs. Carter added a second task to that writing assignment." His teacher asked students to reflect back on their responses to *What kind of world do you want?* Then they were to address a second prompt: *What will you do to make it so?*

"I guess it really was a hopeful assignment, thinking about the power I have to impact change. It inspired me to work in politics and try to make a difference." Matt and I agreed Mrs. Carter's assignment was an exercise in hope. He said that assignment (and Mrs. Carter's passion) inspired him to dedicate his life's work to legislative action aimed at social change.

Critical Hope

As I finished my meal and walked back to my office, I thought about Matt's story. It reminded me of another favorite article perennially pulled out of my overstuffed file and given to students. This article was written by Jefferey Duncan-Andrade, a professor at San Francisco State University who teaches and writes about educational equity. Dr. Duncan-Andrade was once a teacher in Oakland public schools and is a founder of the Roses in Concrete Community School. The school's name pays homage to a line from a Tupac Shakur poem, and this particular article borrows Tupac's metaphor of roses growing in concrete to describe the experiences of urban youth and their teachers. Dr. Duncan-Andrade asserts that hope has always been a theme in movements aimed at social change, and it must be abundantly applied to the education of historically marginalized students.

The article warns against false hope, which can take the form of mythical hope or hope deferred. Mythical hope denies systemic inequities in favor of celebrating individual exceptions. These exceptions are used as evidence that hard work alone leads to a brighter future. Exceptional athletes and scholars are used as proof that the American dream is possible for anyone. However, even the election of Barack Obama (whose platform was largely built on the concept of hope) as President of the United States did not mean that racial barriers had been eliminated. Mythical hope prevents educators from seeing the injustices and suffering that plague many urban students, believing that if students just work hard, they can succeed. Hope deferred does not deny injustice, but it keeps educators from taking action to mitigate inequities. Instead of blaming students for their lack of success, hope deferred is grounded in blaming the system. It is the belief that when society changes, when the economy changes, things will get better, and therefore, we just need to wait.

Dr. Duncan-Andrade is a proponent of critical hope, the kind of hope that sees a brighter future for all as the result of a committed and active struggle. It is the acknowledgement that concrete is not an ideal environment for growth, but as educators, we can find cracks therein to provide resources. If we have the courage to collectively widen the cracks and help students push through, we can create audacious hope. As I walked, it occurred to me that envisioning a better future with our students, finding paths toward that future, and persevering through the struggle is the intersection between Dr. Hellman's research and Dr. Duncan-Andrade's work. Both situate hope in action. Mrs. Carter must have understood that, too. Had she stopped after the first phase of the writing assignment, she may have promoted a falsehood, that hope alone is transformational.

Choosing a Challenging Path

I got back to my office with time to spare before the start of my class. I was teaching about the school improvement process, and in addition to technical skills, I'd been integrating information about the mindset necessary for school improvement. Certainly, hope is necessary for moving a school from its current state to a better future, and so, I decided to include hope in this evening's lesson. And since I am admitting my addictions in this chapter, I will admit that I love TED Talks almost as much as I love research articles. The ability to communicate complicated concepts in under 20 minutes is admirable, and Dr. Hellman's talk on the science and power of hope is no exception. One of my favorite moments is his recollection of a time when he was so distraught that he made a plan for ending his life. A caring teacher reassured him that things would get better and persuaded him to keep going. What power we have as educators! Imagine helping a young person move from hopeless to becoming a seminal hope scholar. I would open my class that evening with Dr. Hellman's talk.

My students are all passionate teachers and aspiring school administrators. They will need ample amounts of hope to sustain and succeed in the challenging work of school leadership. The kind of false hope that denies reality or is naively unaware of the commitment necessary for change won't serve them well. Instead, they need the kind of hope that Mrs. Collins and Mrs. Carter taught and modeled, hope grounded in purposeful action. They are also going to need courage. It takes no courage to maintain the status quo or to expect the worst, but hope rests in the expectation of changing for the better. With that expectation comes the risk of disappointment and discouragement. When all signs point to the impossibility of a dream, it's a risk to continue to hope. Most people need something tangible on which to base their expectations, some evidence of the potential win. But hope requires believing for things yet unseen. Hope requires courage.

Perhaps pausing, pondering, and persisting might also strengthen our hope muscles as educators. Pausing could help us choose optimistic thoughts rather than our default thoughts. Pondering could help us see multiple paths toward a brighter future for our students and ourselves. Persisting could keep us on the path despite the unavoidable obstacles. Charting a new path and staying the course isn't easy. In addition to disappointment, we may experience rejection or ridicule from others. It can be uncomfortable for those around us when we walk in hope and do brave things. It's easier to join the complainers than to step out in hope, but taking action is the way to make an impact.

As I continued to explore turning challenges into opportunities for impact, I wanted to find more examples of educators committed to hopeful action. I wondered how the practices of pausing, pondering, and persisting could increase teacher retention and satisfaction. And I wondered how leaders could support hope-filled cultures in their schools. Soon I would be heading to a conference filled with school administrators. They would surely offer some insight on the courage required to teach and lead from a foundation of hope.

 ## Leveraging the Power of Hope

Pausing with Hope
If we believe that hope is something we do rather than something we have, then we can practice it. Hope is generally not our default response in a difficult situation. We have to choose it, and choosing hope typically requires pausing to push aside an initial unhelpful reaction. When you feel frustrated or discouraged, pause, take a breath, and let yourself imagine a better outcome.

Pondering with Hope
Hope requires a vision of a better future. It may feel like a frivolous activity, but creating a vision is a useful exercise. Give yourself plenty of time to think and reflect on what a better future looks like for you. Ask yourself: *What do I really want? What matters most to me? What makes me feel lighter? What brings me joy?* Your vision can serve as a compass to guide your choices. Once you know where you want to go, you can create a map for getting there.

With your vision in mind, identify goals which can be stepping stones to move you closer to that better future. Choose approach goals rather than avoidance goals. Approach goals are those we want to attain, such as the goal of adopting a regular exercise routine. Avoidance goals are those we don't want, such as not getting an illness. Approach goals are more hopeful.

Persisting with Hope

Goal focused activities often bring new challenges, and you may find yourself getting off track. If you lose focus and let yourself drift, you can end up far from where you want to be. Refocus on your vision often, especially when difficulties arise. Lean on supportive friends and colleagues, and celebrate progress along the way.

 ## Questions for Reflection

When do you feel most hopeful as an educator?
How can you experience more of what brings you hope?
What is your vision of a better future for your profession?
What are potential steps on the path toward that better future?
How can practicing hope help you become a more effective educator?

Notes and Works Cited

Gwinn, C. & Hellman, C. (2022). *Hope rising: How the science of hope can change your life.* Morgan James.

Pharris, A. B., Munoz, R. T., & Hellman, C. M. (2022). Hope and resilience as protective factors linked to lower burnout among child welfare workers. *Children and Youth Services Review, 136.*

Shade, P. (2001). *Habits of hope: A pragmatic theory* (1st ed.). Vanderbilt University Press.

Duncan-Andrade, J. M. R. (2009). Note to educators: Hope required when growing roses in concrete. *Harvard Educational Review, 79*(2), 181–194.

Hellman, C. (2021). *The science and power of hope.* TEDx Oklahoma City.

5

The Power of Courage

I landed in Louisville one day before the start of the National Association of Elementary School Principals annual conference. I was heading to a pre-conference workshop with author and communications consultant Jennifer Abrams, who would provide strategies for successfully navigating hard conversations. My graduate students often lack the skills to navigate hard conversations as they prepare for leadership roles. Their success as leaders depends upon their ability to communicate, especially when it's uncomfortable. We use modeling and role play to practice in class, but even these simulated conversations can go off the rails. I often have one student assume the role of principal while a partner assumes the role of a struggling teacher. Some of the pretend principals quickly launch into the topic of the conversation with little attention to the other person's feelings. After a barrage of criticisms, they abruptly end with a vague directive to just "do better." These no-nonsense, fast-talking students typically come from the northeastern United States, where direct and straightforward communication is the norm. But students from the south approach these talks much differently. Their opening is a long, drawn-out mix of reassurances and "bless your hearts." Somewhere between too soft and too harsh is the sweet spot, and students need help and practice to get there.

Abrams' workshop provided an abundance of information and skill-building activities to share with my students, but it also

DOI: 10.4324/9781003344735-6

prompted me to think about another necessary ingredient for hard conversations: courage. Even with solid tools and preparation, people are tempted to avoid the tension inherent in an honest talk. Abrams offered a list of reasons for hesitating. First, as educators, we tend to be nurturers committed to positive and supportive relationships, and the fear of being disliked or damaging a relationship can hold us back from discussing an issue. And as leaders, we may fear someone retaliating or complaining in response to our conversations. We may also avoid hard conversations to sidestep our own emotional discomfort. Finally, surmising that our efforts won't matter, we may decide the conversation isn't worth risking disruption of the status quo. Certainly, one of our greatest fears as humans is fear of the unknown, and a hard conversation can be unpredictable. We don't know how the other person may respond or the impact of expressing our concerns. All of these fears are valid, but if we are committed to our own growth and the growth of others, summoning the courage to speak up is necessary.

A Life-Shaping Conversation

Abrams provided many opportunities for discussion throughout the workshop, and I frequently engaged with Akeela, who was sitting to my left. Prompted by Abrams' thought-provoking presentation, at one point, we conferred about why it's important to push past our fears and engage in hard conversations. Akeela shared her belief that open and honest dialogue is an expression of care for the other person, and she viewed these tough love talks as a path to impact. Her strong belief was grounded in an experience she had in high school, and she shared the story with me.

"I was a shy kid in high school, and I didn't start dating until the spring of my junior year, when a popular basketball player asked me out," she began. "I think I was so consumed by his attention that I didn't really think about whether the relationship was a good choice for me. He ran with a wild crowd, and I started hanging out with his friends, too."

Akeela described the friends' late-night parties, excessive drinking, and frequent fights. She told me about new troubles in her life, like skipping class and arguing with her parents. She was caught up in a downward spiral but couldn't see the implications.

"That's when Mr. Trask stepped in," Akeela continued while shading in the letters on her handout with a pencil. "He kept me after chemistry class to talk about why my grades had dropped so dramatically. I'm sure he already knew the reason because he'd seen me in the hall several times with my boyfriend. Mr. Trask talked to me about my goals and dreams and about the difficulty of achieving them if I kept going down the path I was on. He said I had great potential, and he didn't want me to risk my future for attention from a boy. He told me I deserved better. Then we made a plan to get my grades—and my life—back on track."

Akeela and I talked about what that conversation meant to her. As an educator herself now, she understood how easy it would have been for Mr. Trask to avoid it. "He cared enough to make the effort, and that conversation changed my life. I think about it every time I need to have a hard conversation with a student, and it inspires me to just do it."

The workshop and the opportunity to talk with Akeela strengthened my belief that problems and challenges are the gateway to impact, but only if we take action. Impactful action often comes in the form of a hard conversation, which requires both skill and courage. Pushing past our own fears and resistance requires caring deeply about the well-being of those we teach and lead. It requires commitment to the long-term well-being of our schools and the people in them. Committing to hard conversations requires staying true to our values and principles. When the workshop ended, I wanted to continue reflecting with my tablemates, but I needed to prepare for my own presentation, scheduled for the first morning of the conference.

Do It Anyway

I wrestled with countless fears the first time I stepped out of a classroom and onto a stage to give a talk. I was comfortable teaching my graduate students, but the thought of speaking to a crowd terrified me. When I was invited to speak at TEDx Eustis in 2019, I knew it was an opportunity to spread a positive message about teaching, but the opportunity came with big challenges. Opportunities for impact usually require us to get to deal with discomfort. Luckily, I found coach Jennifer Samuel-Chance, who helped me develop the competence and confidence I needed to succeed. That TEDx talk became a high point in my life, but preparing for the talk was a journey. You might assume that I conquered my fear of public speaking in that journey, but the truth is, I still deal with fear and anxiety every time I speak.

I suppose my speaking fears are like the fears related to hard conversations: fear of the unknown, fear of failure, and fear of judgment. Even with thorough preparation, a speaker can never really predict how a talk will go. There can be technical difficulties, challenges with the room set up, or the dreaded afternoon energy slump. Speaking right after lunch typically necessitates creative strategies for keeping the group actively engaged. Anticipating all the possible unknowns can mess with a speaker's mind. Thankfully, experience mitigates these fears a bit. While unexpected problems still occur, experience in pivoting and overcoming problems provides reassurance that I can successfully navigate whatever comes. When fear of judgement creeps in, I remind myself that the crowd is pulling for me. They don't want to spend their time watching someone flop on stage. A panicked speaker makes everyone uncomfortable. They want me to do well so that they can learn something new and have a little fun in the process. Focusing on my purpose for speaking and the impact I hope to make is the best way to push fears aside, shifting my focus from myself to others. After all, courage isn't about eliminating fear; it's about acknowledging the fear and doing it anyway.

Tiptoeing around Problems

I woke up early in the morning to go through my pre-presentation routine. The structure and predictability of a routine calms my nerves. And so, I drank my warm lemon water, completed my deep breathing exercises, and recited positive affirmations. When I walked into my assigned room in the conference center, I was relieved to see 20 round tables, a configuration that would accommodate discussion and the sharing of ideas. My session focused on helping teachers feel safe, seen, and stretched as a lever for increased teacher retention. I knew the growing rate of teacher attrition was a concern for principals and wasn't surprised when the seats quickly filled. I shared information and strategies for building trust and psychological safety as well as tools for identifying and utilizing teachers' strengths. The participants were also interested in the responses I had collected from my focus group on teacher retention.

I was surprised by a theme that emerged in the table discussions: Principals were a bit resistant to the notion of helping teachers stretch. With the growing teacher shortage and residual pandemic exhaustion, they felt like they needed to ease up on expectations for professional growth. They were tempted to tiptoe around their teachers for fear of upsetting them, or worse, losing them. I wondered out loud if avoiding hard conversations might ultimately contribute to more teachers feeling unsure about their performance, finding themselves floundering, and ultimately deciding to leave.

Fortunately, Becky spoke up and supported my point. With relief and gratitude, I handed her the microphone.

"An honest conversation and feedback from a principal actually kept me from quitting during my first year of teaching," Becky began as she turned her chair to face the others in the room. "I was struggling with classroom management. I just couldn't get the kids to listen to me. My principal at the time just kept telling me that I would get there and that teaching is hard." She talked about her frustration and thoughts of giving up. "I decided I just wasn't cut out for teaching."

Lucky for Becky, a new principal was assigned to her school halfway through her first year. "Mr. Kline invited each teacher into his office for introductory conversations," she explained. "When he asked how things were going, I just burst into tears. I rambled on about how challenging it was to delay starting lessons or have lessons disrupted because of student behavior." Becky described the patient way Mr. Kline listened. Then he gently asked if he could visit her classroom to observe and offer some suggestions. "I was so nervous about my principal coming in for fear he would think I was a bad teacher, but I was desperate for some help."

"Although the students initially behaved a little better with Mr. Kline in the room, he stayed long enough to see some of the off-task activity." Becky recalled her conversation with the principal after his observation. "He told me that I gave directives that sounded more like questions or suggestions, and that I needed to sound firmer and more decisive. Then he arranged for me to watch an experienced teacher model what he had described." She expressed deep gratitude for Mr. Kline. "If he had just avoided the issue and consoled me instead of gently pushing me to identify the problem and change my practice, I wouldn't be sitting here today." Becky was right. Even during challenging times, teachers still want to stretch and grow.

Like Becky, most teachers appreciate the opportunity to develop their skills and become more effective. Seeing evidence of our own growth can be motivating. But in order to grow, teachers need a clear understanding of their current performance, and communicating openly and honestly about performance takes both effort and courage from a leader. Trying to preserve comfort by avoiding a conversation ultimately works against teacher effectiveness and retention.

The Courage to be Clear

Author and researcher Brene Brown asserts that clear communication is kind. Being unclear about your expectations then blaming someone for not meeting them is unkind. Dr. Brown's assertion supports Becky's point that avoiding hard conversations could ultimately contribute to teachers leaving the profession. Principals may avoid these conversations for fear of losing their teachers' commitment to the school or to their leadership, especially when there are so few candidates to replace them. Many principals also fear their own ability to skillfully navigate a difficult conversation, particularly when emotions are high. Becky's tears surely made Mr. Kline's response a bit more challenging. But according to Dr. Brown, feeding people half-truths to make them feel better (which is almost always about making ourselves feel more comfortable) is unkind. Teachers need honest feedback about their work in order to be successful. Allowing them to continue to struggle is harmful to the teachers themselves and to their students.

One consequence of avoiding hard conversations or uncomfortable interactions is diminished trust. It's difficult to trust those who may be withholding information or only telling us what we want to hear. And distrust ultimately leads to less collaboration and engagement in the work. Teachers are not likely to be open about their struggles with people they don't trust. When we avoid conversations about expectations and accountability, problematic behavior increases, negatively impacting performance. Hard conversations are essential to healthy schools, but they aren't easy. Overcoming the fears that hinder honest communication requires integrity, which means choosing courage over comfort, choosing what is right over what is easy. Hard conversations also require a nonjudgmental stance. When people feel they are being judged, they are less likely to admit mistakes or ask for help.

As the participants in my session and I considered Becky's story and Dr. Brown's work, I could see how pausing, pondering, and persisting were necessary for hard conversations. Pausing gives us the space to become aware of our own emotions and stop an unhelpful reaction. Without a pause, we are more likely to say something we'll regret in the heat of the moment. Pondering allows us to question our narratives, push aside assumptions, and focus instead on the other person's perspective.

Hard conversations are like a dance, with each partner moving in response to the other. It's easy to make a misstep, but through persistence, we can regroup and continue working toward our common goals.

The Courage to be Authentic

When my session ended, I gathered my things quickly so that I could get to a room down the hall to participate in a session on principal actions that ensure equitable outcomes. I found a seat at a table in the back and struck up a conversation with the man seated next to me. Trayvon had recently left his job as a high school principal to become a full-time consultant. He talked about the focus of his work, helping schools develop equitable discipline plans, and I told him about my research on long-term teacher impact. A fellow research aficionado, Trayvon asked great questions and wanted to contribute to my data by sharing a story about a teacher who impacted his life: his high school math teacher, Mr. Atkins.

"I worked hard to earn good grades, and I received a full scholarship to Columbia University," Trayvon began. "It had been my dream to attend a prestigious school, but as it was becoming a reality, I started to have doubts," he explained as he brushed the crumbs from his protein bar off the white tablecloth. "In case you hadn't noticed, I'm a Black man. I grew up in an economically unstable neighborhood, where most people were just trying to get by. I was afraid I would have to abandon part of my identity in order to fit in at Columbia."

My new friend told me it was a stroke of luck that he ended up in Mr. Atkins' calculus class during his senior year. "I learned that Mr. Atkins had graduated from Columbia, and he grew up off Fulton Street in Brooklyn, not far from my home. I could tell right away that he'd held onto his identity." Trayvon described his teacher's t-shirts, sneakers, and the forearm tattoos that represented his childhood neighborhood. "The cool thing about Mr. Atkins was this combination of his Brooklyn identity with who he had become at Columbia. It was like he hadn't completely discarded his roots; Instead, he reflected the totality of his experiences."

Trayvon told me about the many conversations he had with Mr. Atkins, who always advised him to stay true to himself. "He would tell me that pretending to be someone else wouldn't serve me well. My relationships would be inauthentic, and I would lose myself in the end. The way Mr. Atkins embraced and expressed his identity made it feel safe for me to hold onto my own. I realized that going to a new place wouldn't require me to reject parts of myself." I understood Trayvon's gratitude for this enduring lesson. Entering a new community can be scary, and the fear of potential rejection is real. We talked a bit longer about the courage to be ourselves, and we wrapped up our conversation just as the session was starting.

Courageous Teaching

As the day went on, I kept thinking about Mr. Atkins and the courage to be oneself. One of my favorite books, *The Courage to Teach: Exploring the Inner Landscape of a Teacher's Life*, details the importance of revealing parts of our authentic selves in our classrooms. The author, Parker J. Palmer, claims that great teaching comes from the identity and integrity of the teacher. In other words, we teach from who we are, and identity is the intersection of the inner and outer forces that make us who we are. Teaching can be a risky and unpredictable endeavor, and our fear tempts us to take a protective stance and hide our true selves. That stance distances us from students, and it discourages them from opening up and taking their own risks in our classrooms.

So much of our identity as teachers is tied to our work. We care deeply about what we teach and who we teach, and thus, mistakes and missteps hit hard. Few professions have higher highs and lower lows than teaching. The bad days come from struggling at something in which we are deeply invested, something we deeply love. When a lesson doesn't go well, we wonder if we are ineffective teachers. Walking into the classroom every day, we understand the uncertainty of our work. Even as experienced teachers, we carry a smidgeon of fear that we may lose control of the class or fear that we may fail to engage our students. But teaching requires us to push past those fears and show up fully as our authentic selves. When we avoid exploring the depths of our own lives, we can't inspire our students to reflect deeply on theirs. Dr. Palmer proclaims that deep speaks to deep. Real recognizes real, and being real takes courage.

Courage in the Spotlight

On my last day at the conference, I finally ventured out to experience Louisville. I ended up at a table in a courtyard with the city's famous Hot Brown, an open-faced Turkey sandwich topped with cheese, bacon, and Mornay sauce. As I indulged in this local delicacy, I noticed a sign on the stage at the front of the courtyard advertising live music. By the time I had my fill of Hot Brown, the band arrived in a minivan and began unloading their equipment. Unlike most bands you'd find at larger venues, The Most Wanted Band set up the stage themselves, pulling their instruments from the back of a minivan that seemed more suited to folding chairs and coolers of Gatorade for a kids' soccer match than a rock concert. I decided to stick around and see what these women could do.

Turns out, I totally and completely misjudged them. Their set started with a cover of the Loverboy hit, "Working for the Weekend," which made my whole picnic table vibrate. They played everything from Tom Petty to Prince to a haunting version of Radiohead's "Creep," and I watched as the crowd began to grow. People walking through the courtyard stopped to listen. Individuals from different generations and backgrounds danced and sang together for hours. I was moved by the scene and by the women fronting this band. They didn't look like typical rock stars, but that night, they owned the courtyard.

I'd been thinking about courage throughout the conference, and here it was, modeled for me on a stage in the middle of downtown Louisville. It took courage for these atypical rockers to stand in the spotlight and fully immerse themselves in their music, much like the courage Mr. Trask marshaled to talk honestly with Akeela, even though he couldn't predict how she would respond. And it was similar to the courage Mr. Atkins displayed in embracing all aspects of his identity and showing up authentically for his students. Courage is necessary for turning problems into opportunities for impact. But something else is also required: compassion. Courage without compassion can be cruel. I planned to dive deeply into the role of compassion when I got back home. But first, I needed to stop and visit a friend.

 ## Leveraging the Power of Courage

Pausing with Courage

When something goes against your values, you will feel an urge to speak up or stand up, but that urge is usually met with resistance. Speaking up and standing up require the courage to overcome the struggle against doing something uncomfortable. Pause when you feel that urge to act, and notice what emotions come up. Notice the fear and the resistance, and call upon your courage.

Pondering with Courage

Growth requires you to go outside your comfort zone, encounter new situations, and take new actions despite being unsure or afraid. Clarifying your values can help you decide when to push past the fear. Ask yourself, *What do I find intolerable? For what ideals will I take a stand?* Consider how you will feel if you don't speak up. Will you regret your inaction? Consider the possible consequences of speaking up. What is the worst-case scenario? Often, our fears make us project outcomes far worse than reality.

Persisting with Courage

When you have a strong network of colleagues and mentors, you can check in and get advice about when to take action and which actions to take. With a solid network in your corner, you will have better support in a case you stumble. Doing the right thing for yourself and others repeatedly tends to garner respect and rapport, and being consistently courageous is contagious. When you take action in the face of adversity and when you persevere, you contribute to a better future for yourself, your colleagues, and those you teach or lead.

 Questions for Reflection

When are you tempted to avoid having a difficult conversation or taking an uncomfortable action? How can you move past this resistance?

What are your most important values, your nonnegotiables? How do you find the courage to speak up when something violates these values?

How can developing a network of supporters help you push past discomfort and be more courageous?

Notes and Works Cited

Abrams, J. (2009). *Having hard conversations*. Corwin.

Brown, B. (2018). *Dare to lead: Brave work. Tough conversations. Whole hearts*. Random House.

Palmer, P. J. (2007). *The courage to teach: Exploring the inner landscape of a teacher's life* (10th anniversary ed.). Jossey-Bass.

6

The Power of Compassion

The early morning drive out of Louisville provided some uninterrupted time to think about courage. Aristotle once posited that courage isn't just about facing fears themselves, but also the *reasons* for facing them. Our reasons for acting in the face of fear matter, and they can mean the difference between courage, cowardice, and recklessness. Are we acting in the best interest of humanity or in the interest of our own self-preservation? Do we dare to disrupt the status quo for the purpose of lifting others or to be lauded as heroes? Do we take on a fight to make an impact or so that we will be proven right? True courage, according to Aristotle, is to freely choose a battle despite having nothing personally to gain from it aside from the satisfaction of doing what is right and noble. Courage, it seems, can be destructive without compassion.

Empathy involves the ability to take the perspective of and feel the emotions of another person, but compassion includes the desire to help. Compassion is empathy in action. Feeling for the suffering of others without the courage to act can be futile. Compassion requires us to pause and focus on another's needs while questioning how we can help. Compassion also requires persisting through the difficulties of helping someone in need. When we take action in the face of adversity for the purpose of alleviating the suffering of others, we are courageously compassionate. I drove on through the morning thinking about the role of courage and compassion in turning challenges into opportunities for impact.

DOI: 10.4324/9781003344735-7

I planned to stop halfway between Louisville and home to visit my friend, Troy, at Heritage Middle School. Troy is a social studies teacher, but he also teaches an eighth-grade elective called Study Skills. He confessed that much of his time in that class is devoted to everything but how to study. The students placed in the elective have been identified as needing extra support in academics, social skills, emotional regulation, or all of the above. Troy admitted they were a motley crew, but they were without question his favorite class for a lot of reasons, not the least of which was their refusal to do anything just for the sake of compliance. This group required a compelling reason for their effort, and they would jump through no hoop unless deemed important. A grade was not sufficient incentive to complete an assignment; they wanted to know why the learning was important. The rebel in Troy recognized the rebel in them. He loved their lack of pretense, and he loved their rough edges.

Troy asked me to visit his class because he wanted to help the students develop a sense of compassion for their peers and their teachers. They had difficulty seeing how their actions impacted others, and it often led to conflict. He'd been using the stories I shared on the Chalk and Chances website to generate discussion about teachers and teaching. He shared my belief that stories are the foundation of compassion. When students immerse themselves in other people's narratives, and listen carefully with the intent to understand, they begin to identify with others' emotions. They become aware of how other people experience the world. I often talk to teachers and school leaders about my research, but I rarely have the opportunity to talk with young people. I was excited and a little nervous, but I decided to bring all the courage and compassion I could muster into Troy's classroom.

Everybody Hurts

I signed in through the office at Heritage Middle School and arrived in Troy's classroom just as his Study Skills class was returning from lunch. They came in at full speed, each one jockeying to be the first through the door, but Troy quickly settled them down and introduced me. I leaned on the front of Troy's desk, careful not to knock over his cup of pencils. I began to tell them what I had learned about why teachers matter. I told them about my struggle in learning to read in the first grade and the lasting impact of my teacher, Mrs. Russell. The students' nods were affirming, and they seemed to appreciate my openness. I relayed the stories others had shared with me about their teachers, making a special effort to highlight the middle school examples. One story in particular resonated with the students: Jason's story about his sixth-grade art teacher, Mr. Sands.

I told the students that I met Jason at a craft fair where he was selling his oil paintings. When I stopped to ask about the abstract images on his canvases, he told me about his younger years and the impact of his teacher on his life and his art. Jason said his mother left when he was very young, entrusting him to an abusive grandfather. He carried feelings of anger and betrayal, which often manifested in outbursts and fights at school. (It was at this point I sensed some knowing looks on the faces of Troy's students.) I told them about Jason getting kicked out of computer class for destroying a keyboard in a fit of frustration, and how the guidance counselor moved him to an art class instead. Jason recalled meeting Mr. Sands, a long-haired, bearded man who always wore denim overalls covered in paint. Jason remembered how he just sat and scowled the first few days in art class until his teacher said, "Sometimes it's hard to put our feelings into words. That's what paintbrushes are for."

I told the class about Jason's instant sense of release the moment he held a paintbrush and put the first streak of paint on a canvas. I recalled Jason saying to me, "I couldn't wait to get to art class every day. I became totally immersed in my painting and poured all those pent-up emotions onto the canvas. It didn't really matter if the work was good." Then Jason described a very clear memory of Mr. Sands standing in front of one of his finished paintings. His teacher nodded in recognition of the pain represented on the canvas, put his arm around Jason, and softly said, "You're going to be okay." He remembered it as a turning point in his life, the moment when he realized that art was his path forward.

When I finished telling Jason's story, Troy's typically active class sat uncharacteristically still and silent. Finally, a tall girl in the back spoke. "I felt that." Then the boy next to her added, "We all felt that." I sat down in a chair at the front of the room, and Troy joined me. We talked honestly and openly about the pain we all carry, about how everybody hurts sometimes, even teachers. I knew these students were often described as troublemakers. Perhaps they just needed us to understand their stories, and in return, they would try to understand ours.

Troublemakers

It was Troy who first introduced me to the book *Troublemakers*, by researcher and author Carla Shalaby. She studied the experiences of four students identified as "challenging" by their teachers (all deemed effective teachers by their principals). Shalaby intentionally selected students in progressive schools, with teachers lauded by fellow educators, and parents actively engaged in their children's schooling. Even under these ideal conditions, she found structures and procedures that suppressed the students' needs for autonomy and self-expression. Throughout the book, Shalaby revealed the ways these students asserted their own independence and agency against the rules and expectations placed upon them in school. What others might describe as impulsivity, this author redefined as fearlessness. The students refused to comply just for compliance sake, which often frustrated the adults in their lives.

Like these students, many children have a fierce desire to be self-directed, but their school day offers limited opportunities for choice. In school, students are expected to follow directions, work independently, and behave according to long-established norms. Those who do not (or cannot) are often labeled as problem students or troublemakers. Instead of considering the incompatibility between the structure of school and the needs of a child, educators may instead ascribe a pathology to the child. However, the development of future leaders, innovators, and creative problem-solvers will not come from insisting on compliance, but from the encouragement to question existing systems and take risks.The students featured in *Troublemakers* found creative ways to assert their independence, much the same as Troy's students. But unlike some of his colleagues, Troy finds his students' efforts estimable and often amusing. The varied ways they practice creative non-compliance does indicate a certain degree of brilliance. Troy knows his students' stories and understands that their ability to advocate for their own rights and freedoms is the reason many have survived traumatic childhood experiences. Like Jason and his art, some students desperately need the freedom to express themselves and their emotions. These students may find the rigidity of the school day frustrating and repressive. If compassion is grounded in the motivation to help alleviate another's suffering, perhaps the most compassionate thing we can do as educators is to change systems and structures that contribute to the suffering of our students.

Unless You Care

When I finished sharing my research and stories with Troy's class, I invited the students to share their own stories about teachers who impacted their lives. I wasn't surprised when Kaden's hand shot up immediately. He was sitting front and center, and I found it difficult to look away from him while I was speaking. His feet were the only part of him in contact with the seat as he squatted in his chair; his hands were in constant motion as his face shifted into a series of unusual expressions. All that aside, he was clearly engaged in our discussion, and when I invited him to speak, he stood right up next to his desk. He began to talk about his sixth-grade teacher, Miss Nichols.

"I didn't have a lot of friends back then, and some of that was my fault," he said. "You know I like attention, and I would get it in any way I could. I usually came into the classroom shouting so everyone would look at me, and I did some crazy stuff during class."

Kaden spoke about how different Miss Nichols was from some other teachers, how she never yelled and often used humor to diffuse situations. Then he described a conversation he had with her one day after class.

"Miss Nichols told me I was extra, and she liked my energy. But she felt like sometimes I was way too extra on purpose. She thought maybe I was putting on a show so the other kids wouldn't see my true self. Then, if they rejected me, they weren't rejecting the real me." His squirming stopped for a minute and his face grew serious. "Miss Nichols said she had a feeling I was lonely and really did want friends. She told me real friends may hurt me sometimes, but friendship is worth the risk." One of the other students asked Kaden if that conversation hurt his feelings. "Naw, man," he responded. "Teachers don't tell you stuff like that unless they care."

We all affirmed Kaden's statement and agreed that telling people the truth for their own benefit is caring. Like Aristotle suggested, these students believed the reasons behind a teacher's actions mattered. They could sense the difference between actions intended to lift them up and power plays intended to keep them down. I learned so much about courageous compassion from the stories Troy's students shared. Their teachers had sacrificed their own comfort to engage in difficult conversations, to advocate for them against unjust actions, and to apply fair consequences in the interest of their growth. In countless ways, teachers chose to take action in the face of adversity for the purpose of alleviating the suffering of their students.

The Compassion Advantage

Troy had a planning period after his Study Skills class, which he jokingly called his "recovery period." He invited me to stick around for a while. I asked him how he found such satisfaction in working with students who often frustrated his colleagues. My friend confessed that he understands them because he was one of them.

"I grew up in a series of foster homes because my mother couldn't care for me," Troy began. "I knew she loved me, but she was addicted to heroin. When you are young and you have no permanent home or family, you feel untethered. There is no sense of safety or stability." Troy said the one stable force in his life was his second-grade teacher, Mrs. Baker.

"For some reason, she decided to invest her time and energy in me. She interacted with my case worker on a regular basis, and after I moved on from her class, she became a contact on my school emergency card. With the permission of my case worker, she showed up at teacher conferences and advocated for me." Troy described the way Mrs. Baker would appear with gifts on his birthday and holidays. He even spent many holidays and vacations with her family. "Mrs. Baker and her family became the one constant in my life, and knowing I could count on them provided a sense of peace. I still struggled in school when my anger and frustration got the best of me, but Mrs. Baker never turned her back on me."

Troy confided that once he became an adult, he recognized the time and energy Mrs. Baker invested in him. "I told her once that I felt guilty for the time and energy she took from her own family and gave to me. I'll never forget her saying that the opportunity to care for me was a gift. Rather than depleting her, it brought her joy and satisfaction. I don't think I fully understood that until I started teaching."

Troy and I talked about the nature of compassion and the advantages of choosing to be compassionate. Dr. Thupten Jinpa is a former monk, the principal English translator for the Dalai Lama, and the founder of The Compassion Institute. Dr. Jinpa spent decades studying the benefits of compassion, not just for those who need help, but also for the helpers. It seems counterintuitive that acknowledging the suffering of others would lessen our own suffering, but practicing compassion actually reduces our stress and increases our longevity. Compassion shifts our focus from self-judgment and self-consciousness to a sense of connection, something that, as humans, we naturally crave. By considering the humanness of others and helping to reduce their suffering, we feel useful and we realize our purpose. The quality of our relationships is a key determinant of our own well-being and happiness, and healthy relationships are rooted in compassion. Just like Mrs. Baker, we may experience what Dr. Jinpa calls a "helper's high," a mix of positive emotions that accompanies compassionate action.

Dr. Jinpa also acknowledges the need for courage along with compassion. Although we are born with an innate tendency for compassion, we must fight against the forces that pull us in a different direction. Competition and a scarcity mindset can tempt us to prioritize our own power and comfort over helping others. Pursuing what is in our own self-interest can interfere with a compassionate response. We might think that looking out for number one will make us happier, but in the end, it can lead to our own suffering as well as the suffering of others. Compassion provides a moral compass, especially in difficult times. By considering the most compassionate response to a situation, we can make decisions aligned with our own values. We can make decisions we are not likely to regret.

I was grateful for this time with Troy, a friend who models fearless compassion. His story and the stories of his students helped me see the role of compassion and courage in turning challenges into opportunities for impact. I also began to recognize how the courage to be compassionate could bring greater satisfaction to teachers. Rather than depleting educators, these practices could energize us. But while I was clear on the why, I wasn't yet clear on the how. I needed to better understand the moves teachers make when acting with courage and compassion. I thanked Troy for inviting me and headed home to dig a bit deeper into my data.

Compassion in Practice

Back in my home office, I began to look through a stack of stories and pulled out one I had collected on a university campus. The story was shared by Aiden, a medical student who learned about compassion from a high school teacher.

"I took a leadership class with Mrs. Miller my senior year in high school; it seemed like a nice balance to my heavy load of advanced placement classes," Aiden explained. "I expected to learn about giving speeches and getting people to follow my lead, but that was not Mrs. Miller's definition of leadership. Instead, she defined leadership as service to others and emphasized the importance of humility." Aiden described the way Mrs. Miller taught the students how to actively listen and seek first to understand someone else's point of view. Throughout the year, they did service projects for the school and surveyed students and faculty to find out what they needed. "When students complained about the condition of the restrooms, Mrs. Miller asked me to interview the custodian to understand the constraints and appreciate the situation from his perspective." Aiden described it as a formative experience.

"I'm in my last year of medical school now, and those skills have served me well," he said. "There is no shortage of ego among my peers, and many of them forget that their purpose is to serve. I continue to practice active listening with my patients, just as Mrs. Miller taught me. I also keep in mind that I am no better than anyone else on the hospital staff. The truth is, no anatomy or physiology class has had as much impact on me as a physician as that high school leadership class. Because of Mrs. Miller, I approach my work with empathy in addition to expertise."

Looking over the transcript of Aiden's story and my field notes, I thought about the work of Dr. Agnes Wong, a physician and chaplain whose research focuses on the art of compassion in medicine and caregiving. According to Dr. Wong, acting with compassion comprises several elements, including attention, balance, intention, discernment, and engagement. Attention involves training ourselves to notice and recognize the suffering of others. In order to do this, we must quiet peripheral noise and focus on the person in front of us. We must also find our balance by regulating our own emotions and seeing the separation between ourselves and others so that we don't become overwhelmed by their suffering. This can be accomplished by taking a breath and becoming fully present. In other words, the first move in compassionate action is a pause.

By keeping our attention focused on the other person and still seeing that we are separate, we can avoid empathic distress, which may lead us to retreat or to feel frustrated. Instead, we can become intentional about relieving the suffering of another. Being intentional is grounded in understanding our own values and moral obligations. With intention, we act purposefully rather than reacting.

In order to make the right decisions, we must also be discerning. We seek the perspective of the other by asking questions, and we combine that information with our own professional knowledge in order to determine the next right step. In other words, the next move in compassionate action is pondering.

Finally, we remain engaged in the process of relieving suffering. We commit to working through the issues until we find what is helpful, knowing we will encounter challenges and may need to adjust our strategies along the way. And so, the last move in compassionate action is persisting. Suddenly, it became clear. Just like doctors serving patients who are suffering, we can use attention, balance, intention, discernment, and engagement to serve our students in distress. It requires us to pause in order to respond rather than react. It requires us to ponder as we gather information from the student and access our own expertise. It also requires us to persist and continue working through the inevitable obstacles. Pausing, pondering, and persisting are necessary for acting with courage and compassion.

Gentleness and Fire

Thinking of compassion brought to mind my neighbor, Tessa, a gifted baker of bread. She makes countless loaves to share with neighbors in need. There's nothing better than finding one of Tessa's loaves carefully wrapped by the front door. I once asked her the secret to her sundry slices, and she answered with two words: gentleness and fire. The baker must be fully attentive to the mixing and kneading, she advised. Kneading requires both hands and a gentle touch. Otherwise, the dough won't rise. Then, the bread must be baked at precisely the right temperature and time. Nobody likes a crust that is too crusty, she warned.

Tessa's description of turning ingredients into bread reminded me of turning challenges into opportunities for impact in the classroom. Paying attention and responding with just the right touch are necessary for helping a student in need. But without the fire (a.k.a. the courage to take action), we can't alleviate a student's suffering. There are certainly plenty of challenges for educators to address, plenty of opportunities to impact students' lives. But some things remain outside of our control. Spending our energy on things we can't control can be futile and frustrating. Instead, these challenges call for acceptance. I began to wonder how impactful teachers come to accept the things they cannot change. Perhaps I would find some answers in the school district I was preparing to visit next. But first, I needed a warm slice of Tessa's sourdough bread.

 ## Leveraging the Power of Compassion

Pausing with Compassion

Being compassionate requires focusing attention or awareness on others and noticing their suffering. While living a busy life in a noisy world, it is easy to overlook the needs of the people around you. By quieting the mental chatter inside your own head, you can move your focus outward. When you pause and place your attention on others, you are more likely to find opportunities to help.

Pondering with Compassion

Allowing yourself to be moved emotionally by the suffering of others entails trying to understand their experiences. It involves seeking an answer to the question, *What is it like to be the person in front of me right now?* This can be uncomfortable, and you may fear becoming overwhelmed by your own emotions in the process. But if you can simultaneously try to understand the experience of the other person and still see that you are separate, you can be empathetic while avoiding empathic distress.

Persisting with Compassion

When you set an intention to be compassionate, that intention will guide your actions and interactions. An intention helps you to take control of your personal choices and make decisions that align with how you want to live. Setting an intention to notice the suffering of others and take action to relieve that suffering leads to consistently compassionate living. The satisfaction you feel will motivate you to continue leading a life rich in compassion.

 Questions for Reflection

Think about a time you experienced suffering. What compassionate acts were most helpful to you?

How can you set an intention to be more compassionate with your students?

How might that intention be revealed in your actions and interactions in your classroom and school?

What does a classroom or school culture grounded in compassion look like?

Notes and Works Cited

Shalaby, C. (2017). *Troublemakers: Lessons in freedom from young children at school*. The New Press.
Jinpa, T. (2016). *A fearless heart: How the courage to be compassionate can transform our lives*. Hudson Street Press.
Wong, A. (2020). *The art and science of compassion, a primer: Reflections of a physician-chaplain* (1st ed.). Oxford University Press.

7

The Power of Acceptance

Pine Hill County is two hours away from the closest city. Google Maps had given me some indication of its remoteness, but as I approached the county's only high school, its isolation became evident. I did manage to find an open gas station with cold diet soda and a friendly attendant who was curious about why I was in the area. I told him that Trina Taylor, the Professional Development Director of Pine Hill County Schools, had invited me to lead a day of training for their teachers. He welcomed me and offered a complimentary bag of roasted peanuts. Although not my typical breakfast, the soda and peanuts were just what I needed.

I had researched the area as I planned for my work with the school district. Several acres of what eventually became Pine Hill were purchased by a plantation owner in the 1700s. A nearby river and a railroad made the town a busy travel hub in the 1800s. But during Civil War, railroad bridges over the river were burned down, and the canal connecting the river to the town dried up. Those who stayed after the Civil War continued to farm, but these farmers experienced lasting economic hardships. The current population is around 2,000 people, with three-quarters identifying as people of color. The per capita income is below the national average and a third of the population live below the poverty line. Although it is rich in natural beauty, good jobs are hard to find in Pine Hill.

I drove along a winding road between two fields of cotton and into the driveway of Pine Hill High School. Trina was

DOI: 10.4324/9781003344735-8

waiting for me out front to walk me into the lunchroom, which had been decorated with tablecloths, streamers, and balloons in the high school's colors. Trina and I had several conversations leading up to my arrival, and I knew her team put great thought and effort into planning for this day. The school district served a community with a history of economic instability; students and families needed significant support from their schools. Those challenges, combined with the remote location, made it difficult for Trina and the other Pine Hill leaders to attract new teachers to the district—and to keep them. About half of the current faculty and staff were new to the area.

Through our planning conversations, Trina emphasized her goals for the day. She wanted the teachers to be realistic about the challenges but still optimistic about the possibilities. She wanted them to believe they could succeed but also understand that success wouldn't come easy. Trina had gathered many forms of data to provide a picture of the students' current performance. The most recent reading achievement data indicated that only about 20% of their students were currently reading on grade level. Trina and I agreed that this was a pressing issue, and it was an equity issue. The students of Pine Hill County already had many difficulties to overcome, and without reading proficiency, they were less likely to earn a livable wage. In a community composed mostly of students of color, effective reading instruction was a path toward more academic and career opportunities. Trina knew as well as anyone that academic success was a way to a better future.

Through those Doors

On one of our planning calls, I asked Trina what brought her to Pine Hill, and she told me about her own school experience. "Growing up, it was just me and my mom, and things were pretty volatile," Trina began. "My mom was addicted to drugs, which made it hard for her to keep a job. She had a series of boyfriends, and most of them were addicts, too. There were frequent fights, and the police were definitely familiar with our apartment."

Trina told me about how school became a sanctuary for her. "I always loved school. Unlike home, it was stable and predictable. I was probably in fourth grade when I realized that I had no control over what happened at home, but through my focus and effort, I could impact my outcomes at school."

Trina recalled the fourth grade spelling bee, which she entered with the encouragement of her teacher, Miss Eden. "I was afraid to sign up for the spelling bee, certain I would mess up and embarrass myself," she continued. "But Miss Eden insisted, and she promised to help me prepare."

In the weeks leading up to the spelling bee, Trina stayed after school to practice with her teacher. "Miss Eden brought a new list of words every time we practiced, and she also brought me cookies and juice. I loved spending those afternoons with her. She gave me strategies for chunking the words, and I wrote them on index cards to take home and practice."

Trina remembered working through her growing stack of index cards every night. "Even when there was chaos in our apartment, I would find a quiet place to hunker down and practice my words. Focusing on the spelling patterns was a welcome distraction, and through my consistent practice, I was getting pretty good."

Much to Trina's surprise, she won the fourth grade spelling bee. "It was a turning point for me. I realized that I could control the effort I put into my academics, and by putting forth effort, I could determine my destiny."

Trina said when she stepped through those school doors each day, she felt like she could make choices that led her nearer to her goals. She chose to focus her effort on academics and school activities, and that effort was rewarded with a full scholarship to college. Inspired by teachers like Miss Eden, she chose to become an educator. "I want to help kids like me see a path out. I want them to know that they can create their own better future."

After hearing Trina's story, I kept thinking about her words … *through those doors*. As educators, we can't control what happens outside of our schools, but we can control much of what happens the minute we step into our school. We can be intentional about the kind of classroom culture we want to create, and we can make choices aligned with that intention. We can choose how we respond to challenges inside our school. I decided focusing on what we can impact would be the topic of my keynote talk to kick off the day in Pine Hill.

What We cannot Change

The Pine Hill High School Chorus sounded off as the teachers entered the beautifully decorated lunchroom and were seated with their grade level or subject area teams. A Southern-style breakfast—complete with biscuits and plenty of grits—was served by the cafeteria staff and, while everyone ate, the superintendent posed a challenge: Move the percentage of proficient readers from 20 to 50 in the next five years. *Fifty by Five* was the theme of his speech, and it explained the glittery cutouts of the number 50 on each table. Trina spoke next, and she highlighted the professional development initiatives for the coming year. Then she went over the agenda for the day and introduced me.

In honor of the story Trina had relayed to me during one of our planning meetings, I had titled my talk *Through Those Doors*. I asked the teachers to begin by writing their greatest challenges on sticky notes I had placed at their tables. As they finished writing, they stuck their notes on two bulletin boards in the back of the room. One of the boards was labeled "Things Within Our Control," and the other board was labeled "Things Outside Our Control." When all the notes were sorted and placed on the appropriate boards, we began discussing the power of focusing our effort and energy on things we can impact and accepting what we can't. We agreed that we can't control what happens in our students' homes, even though we try to engage parents and provide them with resources. We can't control events that happen in the community and the world, but we have considerable control over what happens when our students walk through the school doors.

My talk included a brief overview of Marsha Linehan's research on radical acceptance. Dr. Linehan is a psychologist and the creator of dialectical behavior therapy, a type of psychotherapy that combines behavioral science with concepts like acceptance and mindfulness. She advocates for radical acceptance, letting go of the illusion of control in favor of accepting things as they are right now, without judgment. Dr. Linehan's research indicates changing our reality first requires accepting it. Rather than being helpful, rejecting reality ultimately contributes to angst and suffering. Refusing to accept reality can keep us stuck in bitterness, anger, and frustration, and although acceptance can bring sadness initially, a sense of peace and deep calm usually follows.

Pain is an inevitable part of life, and resisting what brings us pain leads to unnecessary suffering. That's because the reason for our suffering is usually not the painful experiences themselves, but rather, our interpretations of those experiences. We make bitterness, anger, or frustration more intense through the thoughts and the narratives we generate. Instead of ruminating on the unfairness of a situation, we can learn to accept that, sometimes, it just is what it is. We can accept reality even when we don't find it favorable, and more importantly, we can acknowledge that we don't have the power to change what has already happened. When we practice radical acceptance, we will still struggle with problems, but we won't make things worse by expending our energy resisting what is.

Once we accept what we can't control, we're able to focus our energy and resources on changing what we can. And that is exactly where we directed our focus in the Pine Hill High School lunchroom that morning. One by one, the teachers discussed the challenges they could impact. They couldn't ensure that students would get to school on time, but they could make school an engaging place once students arrived. They couldn't stop violence in the neighborhood, but they could ensure a safe environment within the school walls. They couldn't make sure students ate nutritious meals at home, but they could feed them once they walked through those doors. The school doors were the threshold to what was in their control, and these teachers were determined to direct their attention there, while accepting the things they couldn't change.

Gratitude for What Is

When the opening session ended, the teachers moved into smaller groups for breakout discussions. The topic of my break-out session was how to turn challenges into opportunities in the classroom. Once my first group got settled, I asked the teachers to identify specific challenges they had experienced. As we talked through those challenges, it became clear that their own narratives and assumptions were getting in the way. Many of the teachers came to teach at Pine Hill from other countries, and several in this particular breakout group came from the Philippines. They viewed interactions in the classroom from their own cultural lenses, which were different from those of students raised in Pine Hill. In their culture, many parents made great sacrifices for their children to be educated, and children overcame significant hardships to attend school. They believed having an education opened opportunities that would ensure a good future and eventually lift them out of poverty.

Albert, a math teacher who had come to Pine Hill from the Philippines, often felt frustrated by his students' apparent laziness because they didn't complete assignments. He was raised to view the opportunity to be educated as a privilege and assumed his students took it for granted. I acknowledged his frustration over students not completing their work. We talked about pausing when he felt feelings of frustration emerging, then we engaged in pondering. As a group, we brainstormed other possible reasons for not completing work. Did students lack efficacy in math? Did they lack foundational skills? Were troubles in their lives making it difficult to focus? As we continued to work with Albert on turning his challenge into an opportunity for impact, he filled his notes page with questions and wonderings.

Ana, who had also recently come to Pine Hill from the Philippines, asked if she could share an example of how one of her teachers leveraged a challenge to make a lasting impact on her life. Like her students, Ana understood how it felt to grow up without sufficient financial resources while dreaming of a better future. "I walked many miles to get to school, and during the rainy season, I had to walk on flooded roads. The snakes came out when it flooded, but I was more concerned about ruining my only pair of shoes," Ana began. She explained how she often wrote and drew pictures of her future and her dream of coming to the United States. "I imagined beautiful houses, restaurants, and stores full of shoes. I couldn't wait to get here. But my teacher, Miss Sanday, was worried that I was missing the joy in my childhood by longing to be grown. And so, she told me to find one beautiful thing on my way to school each day. She would ask me about my one beautiful thing when I arrived every morning."

Ana explained how she started looking for beautiful flowers and listened for the birds singing on her way to school every day. She found beauty in the mountains and rivers and in the smiles of her neighbors. "I began to appreciate my home. I found beauty amid the difficulties. I learned to accept and to enjoy my life as it was even as I worked to create a better future for myself."

Ana then shared how she uses gratitude journals with her students in Pine Hill. "Because of Miss Sanday, gratitude became a lasting practice in my life. I want to help my students find joy even through their struggles. So, I ask them to find one beautiful thing each day," she said. "Many of them have cameras on their phones, and they take pictures of the beauty they find. We compile the pictures in a digital collage. I want them to learn to appreciate this place even when they dream of being someplace else."

Our breakout session group marveled at the way Ana carried a lesson from her childhood teacher into her own classroom thousands of miles away. We talked about the way young people tend to be someplace else in their minds, but teachers can help them wake up to the beauty of the world around them. Their rejection of what is and constant longing for something better keeps them from noticing and appreciating their current reality. Teachers can help them see that life doesn't exist in a future destination; what is happening in the present moment is life. And despite the challenges in existing conditions, there is always beauty to be found.

Gratitude and Acceptance

Kristi Nelson is the Executive Director of A Network for Grateful Living and a long-time stage IV cancer survivor who supports others in living with gratitude. She describes gratitude as a practice that we can build through daily repetition. Common attitudes, such as resentment, frustration, and worry, can easily become practices we engage in automatically. By becoming aware of these habits, we can interrupt them and replace them with something more peaceful and productive. Nelson acknowledges that our goal is not to live in a constant state of gratitude, but to learn to use gratitude as a touchstone to regain awareness and shift our perspectives.

While it is difficult to be grateful in the midst of challenges, we can learn to see that the gift in any given moment is opportunity. Like Nelson, those who have navigated life changing illnesses and injuries learned to accept what is and found gifts in the struggles. They found opportunities to develop inner strength and forge deeper connections with friends and family. Our troubles can take up all the space inside our minds and create a considerable racket, making it hard to notice the quieter voice of opportunity. Practicing gratitude helps us learn to listen for the opportunity in every moment. Nelson suggests that when challenges arise, we stop, look, and go. First, we stop to breathe and notice what is happening in the moment. Then we look to become aware of what is going on around us while reminding ourselves that life is a gift and full of opportunities. Finally, we go and take action that reflects this awareness and grateful perspective.

Nelson proposes that gratitude and acceptance are a powerful combination. Accepting and being grateful for what is does not mean that we stop trying to improve. We live in an ever-changing, ever-evolving world that invites us to acknowledge the current reality while also seeing the possibilities for a better future. Acceptance anchors us so that we might focus on the present rather than aimlessly drifting in wishing, dreaming, and pining for anything other than what is. Gratitude helps us appreciate the beauty and see the opportunity in the present moment. By pausing and pondering, we can ask, *What is happening right now in my life and in the world?* Then we can consider, *What can I do to make it better?* This is the lesson Miss Sanday taught Ana. Life is simultaneously full of struggle, beauty, and opportunity.

Accepting Our Individuality

When the sessions had ended for the day, I packed up my rolling laptop bag and headed down the hall toward the parking lot. On the way, I bumped into Arturo Azara, the director of the Pine Hill High School Chorus. I told him how much I enjoyed the group's performance at breakfast, and he responded in kind by complimenting my keynote. He admitted that my talk inspired him to think about his favorite teachers, especially his high school chorus teacher, Mr. McCain. As usual, I invited him to share his story.

"I was not the greatest singer, but I loved to sing," Arturo began. "While I had good volume and control, my pitch wasn't always perfect." Arturo confessed that he was reluctant to even try out for chorus. "I finally got up the nerve and auditioned with 'Stand by Me,' one of my favorite songs. When I finished, Mr. McCain said that I was off on a couple of notes, but he loved my phrasing and the emotion I conveyed."

Arturo explained how his teacher consistently offered a combination of praise and critique in response to his performances. "Mr. McCain helped me recognize my own strengths and needs rather than comparing myself to others. I learned that singing is a complex task, and nobody does all the components perfectly. More importantly, I learned that the combination of my strengths and weaknesses are what make me a unique performer. Because of that lesson, I try to help my own students accept themselves as singers (and as humans) as they are while still continuing to grow."

Arturo finished the story just as we reached the doors to the parking lot. He held a door open for me, and I wished him all the best with his students. "Don't you worry," he called after me. "I plan to focus my energy on what happens when my students come through these doors every day."

Self-Acceptance

As I loaded my bags into the back of my car and closed the hatch, I thought about Arturo's story and the power of self-acceptance. Michael Bernard, a professor and expert in social-emotional wellbeing, identifies self-acceptance as one of the most important attributes underpinning mental health. Practicing self-acceptance requires a realistic awareness of our strengths and weaknesses. It involves acknowledging imperfections and understanding that we can stumble and still reach our goals. When we understand and accept ourselves, it is easier to avoid comparisons with others and resist taking their judgment personally. When we accept ourselves, we're able to embrace all parts of ourselves unconditionally. We acknowledge our strengths and capabilities as well as vulnerabilities and limitations.

Accepting your imperfections does not mean excusing your own behavior when it is harmful to yourself or others. In fact, self-acceptance is an empowering stance from which to make a change. It starts with distinguishing between yourself and your behavior. There is a big difference between making a mistake and *being* a mistake, between failing at a task and being a failure. It is also important to become aware of the automatic tape that plays in your head. Becoming cognizant of your habitual thoughts can help you replace unhelpful messages with those that are helpful and true. Accepting yourself and standing in your power isn't possible without dropping the weight of unconscious thought patterns that no longer serve you. Teachers like Mr. McCain help us break unhelpful patterns and grow toward our potential.

Joy and Pain

I connected my phone to the stereo system as soon as I got into the car. I had downloaded the audio book *The Princess Bride* for the drive home. In this recording, the story is read by Rob Reiner, who directed the motion picture based on the classic tale. In case you are unfamiliar with the story, it centers on Buttercup, a former farm girl chosen to be the princess bride to Prince Humperdinck of Florin, whom she despises. Buttercup is still lamenting the death of her one true love, Westley, a hired hand on the farm before seemingly being killed by the Dread Pirate Roberts. Out on a horse ride to distract herself from the upcoming wedding, Buttercup is kidnapped by bandits. Buttercup and her kidnappers find themselves pursued by the Dread Pirate Roberts (who—spoiler alert—turns out to be Westley). Prince Humperdinck (to whom Buttercup is now betrothed) is also trying to get her back but seems to care little for her well-being or survival. Through swordfights, monsters, and a litany of terrible circumstances, Buttercup and Westley finally prevail.

Despite my commitment to consuming this audiobook just for enjoyment, I managed to make several connections to my research while listening. One of the most prevalent lessons in this whimsical fairy tale is life isn't fair. Sometimes bad things happen to good people. It is important to acknowledge this truth and keep moving forward. At one point in the story, Buttercup accuses a disguised Westley of mocking her pain, and he eloquently replies, "Life is pain, your highness. Anyone who says differently is selling something." Buying into the narrative that we should not feel discomfort or pain or that we should not have problems contributes to our suffering. Rather than resisting circumstances beyond our control, we can learn to accept what is and find a way to continue moving forward. And in the end, our problems might just be the path to a happier ever after.

As educators, accepting the challenges inherent in our current reality while still identifying opportunities for improvement can lead to greater peace and productivity. Often, what wears us down is the energy we spend pushing against that reality and wishing circumstances were different. Practicing acceptance of what is and gratitude for the opportunities within our challenges requires us to be fully present in the moment, not thinking about the future or ruminating about the past. I was interested in learning more about how educators stay present, and I knew my friend, Maria, would have some insight. Maria is the director of an early childhood center, and nothing can pull us back into the present moment better than a young child. And so, as soon as the audiobook ended, I called my friend to schedule a visit.

 ## Leveraging the Power of Acceptance

Pausing with Acceptance

When you are struggling with a problem, it is natural to want that problem to just go away. However, rejecting reality can make a problem worse, and it also blinds you to the opportunities hidden within a problem. Instead of using your energy to resist what is, you can use your energy to identify what you can impact. Acceptance requires becoming aware of what is happening in the moment, accepting what is without judgment, and identifying the opportunities hidden in the challenges. Pausing to consciously acknowledge your thoughts and feelings in the midst of a challenge is the first step toward acceptance.

Pondering with Acceptance

Then you can be curious (yet compassionate) about how your thoughts, feelings, and behavior are helping or hindering you in a challenging situation. It is normal to be frustrated, sad, or grieving, but staying in those feelings for too long can keep you from moving forward. You begin to move forward when you accept what you can't change and focus your energy on what you can impact. You can ask: What are my thoughts and feelings about the situation? What is within my control? What actions would move me toward a more empowered place?

Persisting with Acceptance

Acceptance of the current reality is key to shifting from resistance to persistence. When you do not accept the current situation, you may be using your precious energy to actively resist it. Acceptance is a practice, and you can choose to consistently take steps to limit your automatic resistant reactions in the face of challenges. When you can fully accept what is happening now, you can begin to create new opportunities for yourself and your colleagues, students, and community.

 Questions for Reflection

Think of three things in your current professional context that you are tempted to reject or push against rather than accept. Why are these things difficult for you to accept?

What challenges in your work are outside of your control? How can you focus your energy on what you can impact?

How can you accept yourself just as you are while still committing to continuous improvement and growth?

Notes and Works Cited

Linehan, M. (2021). *Building a life worth living: A memoir*. Random House Publishing Group.

Nelson, K. (2020). *Wake up grateful: The transformative practice of taking nothing for granted*. Storey Publishing, LLC.

Bernard, M. (2013). *The strength of self-acceptance: Theory, practice and research*. Springer.

8

The Power of Presence

While it was still dark outside and I was pouring my first cup of coffee, my phone buzzed with a text message from Maria Flores: *Looking forward to seeing you today. Don't wear your good clothes, the ones that have to be dry cleaned. And leave your grown-up shoes at home, too.* My friend knew me well, and I headed downstairs to select a different outfit. Once appropriately dressed in khaki cropped pants, a comfortable sweater, and sneakers, I drove toward the Hayes Early Learning Center. Visiting the center and Maria (who's been the center's director for nine years) is always a heartening experience. Some places just feel good when you walk inside, and the center is one of those places. From the garden out front to the rainbow mural that surrounds the front door, it draws you in.

The receptionist buzzed me in, and Maria came to the front office to greet me. As usual, she was wearing running shoes. This particular pair was bright yellow with blue laces, a favorite among her many pairs. I once asked her why she wore sneakers, and she told me it was so she would always be ready to play. If a child asks her to jump rope while she is walking through the playground, she is ready to jump in. If a chance to dance is presented in a classroom, she already has on her dancing shoes. It's this spontaneity that I admire most about my friend. She doesn't try to predict what might happen and prepare accordingly. Instead, she is ready for whatever comes, fully present in each and every moment.

DOI: 10.4324/9781003344735-9

Being Present

Being present means being aware and mindful of what is happening right now, not distracted by ruminations on the past or worries about the future. Ellen Langer, a professor and psychologist at Harvard University, researches the importance of mindfulness in living a satisfying life. According to Dr. Langer, mindfulness is the process of actively noticing new things, which keeps us in the present moment. This noticing makes us more outward-focused, more sensitive to context and perspective, and more engaged. Dr. Langer asserts that being mindful is energy-begetting, not energy-consuming. People often assume that staying attuned to what's happening in the moment is stressful and exhausting. However, stress is more likely to come from letting our minds automatically default to a worry and rumination loop.

Dr. Langer asserts that stress is not a function of an event; rather, it's a function of the view we take of the event. If we think something is going to happen and the consequences of it will be awful, we feel stressed. Trying to predict what is likely to happen is pointless. We tend to use our past experiences to predict an outcome, but we can't ever really know what will occur. Instead, we can stay open to all the possibilities by staying in the present moment. Then we can respond to what is actually happening instead of feeling anxious about the future or frustrated about the past. Focusing our attention in the present moment also helps us take in information and make thoughtful choices. Mindfulness helps us realize that there are no better or worse outcomes, just countless different possibilities, each with its own challenges and opportunities. Being mindful is just like Maria wearing her running shoes. When we show up ready for anything, we can dance with whatever the day brings. And this day at the center was sure to bring some joyful surprises.

Being Playful

I followed Maria on her morning walk through the center, and our first stop was Colin Gregory's pre-kindergarten classroom.

This classroom had a happy buzz, with children engaged in different activities and Mr. Gregory circulating among them. With so many conversations and activities, it initially looked a bit chaotic, but closer inspection revealed serious learning happening. Each student had a clipboard with a schedule for the rotation of learning centers. Some of the centers were structured with puzzles to complete or letters to trace. Others provided more choice, with art supplies or props for role-playing. Children were problem-solving, pivoting through mistakes, and negotiating taking turns with their peers. As I walked through the classroom, I began to identify the many different skills students were practicing. They were using fine motor, gross motor, cognitive, oral language, sensory-motor, critical thinking, and social skills all in the context of play.

I stopped by a group of three young students working on a big, floor puzzle. They had 19 pieces in place with one open space and one puzzle piece left. But this group had a problem: One piece didn't seem to fit into the one remaining space. The three friends began to look frustrated until one spoke up. "Wait … Let's take a step back and look at it again," she said. They stood up, stepped back, and examined their puzzle from above. They wondered out loud if the other pieces were correctly placed and agreed that they seemed to be. Then they decided to try flipping the piece upside down. Like magic, the last piece slipped into place. The three friends celebrated, and Mr. Gregory (who had been watching from across the room) came over to give each a high five. It occurred to me that these students had just perfectly modeled my own framework. When they felt frustrated, they paused. Then they looked at the situation from a different angle and pondered. They persisted until their problem turned into a celebration of success. We could learn much about pausing, pondering, and persisting from young children, I thought.

After circulating for a few more minutes, I sat down next to a student in a make-believe office setting. He was answering a play phone and writing messages on a pad of paper. Delighted to have a visitor in his office, he pretended to answer the phone then handed it to me. "It's the President of the

United States," he announced. Of course, I answered the President's call and told him that teachers need salary increases, more support, and an endless supply of free coffee. Just as I finished role playing with my young friend, the teacher assistant rang the bell for the students to clean up and prepare to go outside.

Teaching in the Moment

After the last student left and the classroom grew quiet, Maria introduced me to Colin and told him about my project. We talked a bit about his choice to become an early childhood educator, and he revealed that this choice was inspired by his high school teacher, Mrs. Guthrie.

"My sophomore year in high school was difficult," Colin explained. "My parents were going through a contentious divorce, and I was in the middle. I worried about them all the time, my mother especially. And I worried about what my future would be like with all the upheaval. That's when I met Mrs. Guthrie."

Colin admitted a girl who sparked his interest signed up for Mrs. Guthrie's Child Development class, and he decided to follow her lead. "Little did I know how much that class would impact my life," he said. "Monday through Thursday each week, we had about a dozen young children to care for and teach. The seniors (who had already taken the first two levels of Child Development) designed lessons and activities, and the sophomores assisted. On my first day, I had no idea what to do. Mrs. Guthrie kept encouraging me to just get down on the floor with the children and play."

Colin described how the chance to play brought joy back into his life. "Whenever I sat down to help a child build a tower out of blocks or cook pretend soup in a pot, I forgot all about the stress of my home life. It was impossible for my mind to be anywhere else but right there."

He stayed in Mrs. Guthrie's program for the next three years. "By the time I was a senior, I was planning lessons. I loved the challenge and creativity in planning how to teach skills through play. I knew I wanted to make teaching my career. It's what makes me feel most alive."

"Even now," Colin confessed, "When I'm going through a difficult time, I forget all my problems the moment I walk into the classroom. When my students are here, I can't be anywhere else but here with them."

I knew exactly what Colin meant. As a former kindergarten teacher myself, watching my young students make new discoveries made me look at the world in new ways, too. And even now with my graduate students, when I am fully present in class, all my worries and ruminations disappear. While the students are making discoveries about teaching and leading, they're helping me look at my profession through fresh eyes. Just as Dr. Langer suggested, noticing new things with them keeps me firmly in the present moment. With so many distractions right in the palms of our hands, it can be difficult to focus on the people in front of us. But as Colin's story of his experience in Mrs. Guthrie's class illustrated, being present leads to greater happiness.

Savoring the Moment

Sonja Lyubomirsky is a psychologist and professor at the University of California who researches the benefits of happiness. According to Dr. Lyubomirsky, it's human nature to want greater happiness, and when we aren't happy, we may seek happiness in unhelpful or unhealthy ways. Many people assume that a future state is the key to greater happiness. If we could just achieve more success, better relationships, or better health, we would be happier. But Dr. Lyubomirsky suggests that these achievements are the result of happiness, not its cause. The key to happiness does not lie in the future. Instead, we can find more happiness by staying right here in the moment. When we habitually think about future moments, we fail to enjoy and savor what is happening now. By allowing our minds to always be someplace else, we miss out on the goodness in our lives. Just as Colin discovered in Mrs. Guthrie's class, waking up to what is happening in the present moment can reduce stress and boost happiness.

Dr. Lyubomirsky recommends seeking moments of flow and savoring pleasurable moments as strategies for becoming more present and increasing happiness. Moments of flow happen when we are so immersed in an activity that we lose track of time and lose any sense of self-consciousness. We do something for the sheer love of it and enjoy the challenge of getting better at it. Much like the experience of flow, savoring happens when we prolong enjoyment, when we slow down and notice the pleasure in ordinary moments. When we practice savoring, we intensify those moments. Slowing down to savor a hot cup of coffee or a chat with a friend can heighten those simple pleasures and boost happiness. Staying in the moment by admiring beauty wherever we find it can help us feel happier and more fulfilled.

The Power of Play

Maria and I eventually made our way out to the playground where the students were circled around the edges of a multi-colored, nylon parachute. The children held onto the edge of the parachute and lifted it when directed by the teacher assistant. Each time it caught the breeze, the designated student called the names of two friends who ran underneath and sat giggling in the middle of the circle as the parachute floated back down. Maria and I found our own spots around the edge, and the student excitedly called our names. We ran into the center and quickly sat down as the parachute softly collapsed over us. Once the students realized everyone had been to the center at least once, they knew their favorite part of the game was about to happen. The parachute lifted, and the designated caller yelled, "Everyone!" All at once, 15 students and 3 adults scurried to the middle of the circle as the parachute came down. We all sat covered by the nylon fabric, laughing and cheering, until we finally made our way back out from underneath.

I couldn't remember the last time I allowed myself to play, and I had no idea how much I needed it. Stuart Brown, a psychiatrist and the founder of the National Institute for Play, suggests that play is critical for healthy social relationships, creativity, innovation, and overall well-being. As adults, we often give up play in favor of productivity and efficiency, not realizing that play may be the key to our success. We mistakenly think activities which can't be directly tied to measurable results are frivolous, but seemingly unproductive activities are what help us stay engaged in our work. Without play, our work (and our lives) can become transactional and soulless. Play reignites the spark that keeps us awake and alive.

According to Dr. Brown, play is difficult to define, but it has some distinct attributes. First, it is not done for a practical purpose. Play is done for its own sake, for the sheer pleasure it brings. Play is voluntary, and when it feels like an obligation, it loses its appeal. Play also produces psychological arousal; it stimulates our brains and gets us excited. And play provides a sense of escape. Like a flow state, we lose track of time when we get lost in play. One of the most attractive aspects of play is diminished self-consciousness. When we are playing, we don't worry about looking silly. With its improvisational potential, play opens us up to serendipity and chance occurrences leading to new discoveries and creative ideas. Taking time to play allows us to momentarily shake off constraints and the things that tie us down so that we can feel more free.

Joining that parachute game made me reflect on the importance of bringing aspects of play into my work as a teacher and researcher. Loosening up the rules and constraints (many of which are self-imposed) would surely make me happier and more creative. Do I really need to follow the same structure every time I plan a lesson? And do I need to stick to the lesson plan when an unexpected teachable moment arises? As a researcher, does following the rules and traditions of qualitative research keep me from seeing creative ways to collect, analyze, and share data? Bringing a playful approach to my work could open up new possibilities, and it would surely benefit my students, too. We all like to have fun, and incorporating some play into our teaching can make class more enjoyable for everyone.

Choosing to Play

After walking through a few more classrooms, Maria and I headed back toward the office. I shared my new commitment to bring more play into my work, and then she shared a story I hadn't heard before. "In all our years of friendship and collaboration, I don't think I ever told you about the teacher who impacted me most as an educator," Maria began. "You know that my parents immigrated to the United States when I was a baby. They worked very hard to provide for me and scraped together enough money to send me to a religious school, which was important to them." Maria explained the school's uniform policy and shared that her family could only afford one uniform and one pair of school shoes. "Every day, they told me to keep my uniform clean and not to ruin my school shoes, and so, I sat on a bench while the other kids played on the playground."

With her parents' strict work ethic, Maria said she had never been encouraged to play. "That changed in Miss Nunez's second-grade class," Maria revealed, stepping up to the water fountain to fill her reusable bottle. "Miss Nunez somehow deduced that I was afraid of ruining my school clothes, so she brought in an extra pair of tennis shoes her daughter had outgrown. Every day before recess, she let me change into those shoes, and she put a smock over my uniform. I got to run and play with the others, and it made me feel so free."

Maria explained how her year with Miss Nunez inspired her to make play a continuing part of her life. "As an educator, I am committed to giving students ample time to play and explore.

And as a parent, I strive to make time to play with my kids every day. I've realized that play isn't just good for the kids, it's good for me. It keeps me from getting stressed out over the little things. It keeps me from being too much in my own head. Just like it did in Miss Nunez's class, taking time to play still helps me feel free and alive."

Maria's story made me think of a favorite quote: *"Be where your feet are."* A tenant of many religions, this quote is a favorite of Scott O'Neil, former CEO of the Philadelphia 76ers. In his book, aptly titled *Be Where Your Feet Are*, O'Neil explores the concept of opportunity cost. It's borrowed from microeconomics, and it means that in every activity we choose to pursue, we lose the value and benefits we'd gain from an alternative activity. In other words, every time we choose something, we give up something else. The key to a successful life is to choose thoughtfully and in alignment with your values. And once you choose, be all in on that choice. When you choose to play with your kids, don't let your mind be on the work you need to finish. When you choose to be engaged in work, don't let your mind wander to other places. According to O'Neil, the most important moment in life is the present moment, and we should nurture and appreciate its uniqueness. After all, it's the succession of meaningful moments that add up to a meaningful existence. By missing the moments through distraction or worry, we miss our lives. I talked with Maria about this concept as we walked back to the front office, then I thanked my friend for the soul-restoring hours and promised to come back soon.

A Tale of Two Teachers

Since I was already wearing comfortable shoes, I had no excuse to skip my daily walk, and so, I stopped at the Valle Crucis Community Park, a short distance from home. This beautiful (and unusually warm) day had drawn many people to the park, and as I progressed along the walking track at its perimeter, I witnessed some kids begin a spontaneous game of tag in the field with a large golden retriever determined to join them. Several people were fly-fishing in the river, and a group with a birdwatching guide was exploring the trees along the shore. I noticed how absorbed they all were in their chosen activities, completely oblivious to me watching them from the walking track.

Observing these park visitors, I couldn't stop thinking about the importance of play in teaching and learning. I began to consider teachers from my past who brought a playful presence into the classroom. Dr. Daigle, my college physics professor, came to mind. I had taken physics in high school and didn't enjoy it. The teacher would copy full sections of the textbook onto overhead transparencies, then had us copy from the overhead into our notebooks while he read the notes out loud. It was the ultimate exercise in compliance. He would get visibly agitated (with a red face and a furrowed brow) when a student asked a question. I clearly remember the clock on the front wall of his classroom. I watched the minute hand slowly move around that clock every day until the hour finally ended.

When I started my first semester of college, my classes were already assigned by my advisor. I was disappointed to learn that I had physics on Monday and Wednesday afternoons, but that class could not have been more different than the one I'd taken in high school. Dr. Daigle wore sneakers and cardigans every day, and he practically bounced when he introduced a new concept. I remember him asking for a volunteer to stand by as he swung buckets of water around to demonstrate centrifugal force, promising he wouldn't splash a drop. And I have a clear recollection of him swinging back and forth on a giant pendulum. He loved questions and encouraged curiosity. He played with the laws of physics, and we all had fun. I finally learned the concepts I had copied in my notebook the year prior—and I couldn't even tell you where the clock was in Dr. Daigle's room.

Without a playful presence, we can get in the habit of sleepwalking through the school day. We can easily reduce acts of intellect, creativity, and problem-solving to meaningless tasks. Focusing on compliance and just going through the motions can become all too common. By the time we've been in school for more than a few years, we tend to lose the intellectual engagement so evident in the students at the Hayes Early Learning Center. But if we can fight that temptation, and choose instead to remain curious and intellectually engaged, we will find more meaning and satisfaction as teachers and as learners. Dr. Daigle understood that. In honor of him, as I walked through the park, I recalled the properties of physics underlying the bikes, kites, and frisbees I observed.

Waking Up

With its constantly changing landscape, it's easy to notice new things at the park. In the spring, daffodils sprout up through the soil, tiny green leaves appear on trees, and the robins return to poke around for worms. When spring turns to summer, the fields are alive with wildflowers. By fall, the flowers fade, and the trees are ablaze with colorful leaves. When the last of the leaves fall, the bare branches sag a bit with the weight of the snow. Every season brings its own scenery and its own versions of play. Hiking and canoeing in the warmer months is replaced by skiing and tubing in the winter. If there was ever a place custom made for being present, it's the North Carolina high country. But even here, I find myself sleepwalking through my life far too often.

What if I approached each day like the students at the early learning center? What if I committed to staying alert and noticing new things? It would just require paying attention and being intentional. Staying present would certainly help me notice opportunities for impact. Staying open and playful would also help me generate new ways to turn problems into opportunities. Dr. Daigle had shown that presence and playfulness exists far beyond the early childhood center, and I would soon have a chance to test that idea out. I had volunteered to assist at

Rockville High School's Innovation Day, and I couldn't wait to see the students' projects.

 ## Leveraging the Power of Presence

Pausing with Presence

When you are struggling with a problem, you can make the problem more difficult by shifting your attention to what happened in the past or what might happen in the future. These ruminations or anxious thoughts cause unnecessary stress as you can't change the past or predict the future. Peace and productivity lie in dealing with the moment as it is happening, but being fully present takes practice. The best place to start is just noticing your surroundings. Notice the physical features of whatever space you are in, notice the colors, shapes, and patterns. Close your eyes and notice the sounds. Notice the parts of your body in contact with something solid, like your feet on the ground or your body in a chair.

Pondering with Presence

You might believe you are more productive when working on several tasks at one time, but multi-tasking actually makes you less productive. Instead of trying to juggle multiple things, ask yourself, *What is most important in this moment?* When you determine what is most important, you can devote all your energy to that priority. Not only will you be more productive by limiting your focus, you will more clearly remember the details of the moment.

Persisting with Presence

Life is full of distractions, and sometimes your mind wanders. Instead of judging yourself, you can simply redirect your focus back to the important task at hand. You can also incorporate practices that train your mind to be more present. Taking a few minutes throughout the day to just focus on your breathing can help center you and improve focus. And savoring each meal and each conversation helps train your mind to stay focused. Most importantly, taking breaks from technology and social media can help you stay in the present moment. You may think these tools and apps keep you more connected, when in fact, they can bring distractions that make you less connected. Living in the present moment requires effort to appreciate where you are, what you're doing, and who you're with. But it's this effort that will help you find more opportunities to make an impact.

 Questions for Reflection

What are the greatest distractions keeping you from staying focused on the present moment? Do these distractions typically come from inside (your thoughts) or from outside (your phone)? How can you limit these distractions?

When are you tempted to multi-task? How might multi-tasking impact your performance and your well-being?

How could staying fully present in each moment improve your productivity and your relationships?

Notes and Works Cited

Langer, E. (2014). *Mindfulness* (25th anniversary ed.). Da Capo Lifelong Books.

Lyubomirsky, S. (2021). *The how of happiness: A practical guide to getting the life you want.* Piatkus.

Brown, S. (2010). *Play: How it shapes the brain, opens the imagination, and invigorates the soul.* Avery.

O'Neil, S. (2023). *Be where your feet are: Seven principles to keep you present, grounded, and thriving.* St. Martin's Essentials.

9

The Power of Rethinking

I'd been anticipating my day at Rockville High School since I received the invitation from Amari Jackson to assist with their Innovation Day. Four years ago, Amari, a former student of mine, was appointed principal and found himself with multiple challenges to tackle: low attendance rates, low achievement scores, and lack of community support. Identifying student connectedness and student engagement as root causes, he began to examine these issues and search for strategies that could support improvement. School connectedness is the degree to which students feel accepted, respected, and included in the school community. Engagement is the discretionary attention and effort students apply in the classroom and school. In other words, connectedness is how students feel at school, and engagement is what students do there. Amari knew firsthand how focusing on these two areas could positively impact students and the school.

Amari had been one of my graduate students, so I already knew about the teacher who helped him feel connected and engaged. As I typically do in class, I had asked about what inspired my students to become educators, and Amari quickly volunteered to share a story with his fellow students and me about Mr. Martin.

"I was not into school and thought about dropping out as soon as I could," he began. "I didn't care about academics, and I usually sat in my classes writing rhymes for rap songs.

DOI: 10.4324/9781003344735-10

My English teacher, Mr. Martin, found a paper I dropped on the floor one day and asked me about it." Amari admitted he thought he'd get a referral (some of the lyrics were not exactly school appropriate), but instead, Mr. Martin revealed his own passion for hip-hop.

"From that day on, my teacher recommended old-school rap songs to me, everything from Eric B. to Public Enemy. And I shared some of the new stuff I was into with him. It was the first time I really felt a connection with a teacher," Amari acknowledged.

In addition to teaching English, Mr. Martin was also the Poetry Club Sponsor. "He convinced me to come to a meeting and try it out," Amari continued. "The kids in there were writing and sharing all kinds of poetry, and some of them were doing spoken-word stuff with rhythm and rhyme. I began to meet with a small group of them at lunch in Mr. Martin's room to collaborate." Amari told us that he started to look forward to school. His attendance and grades improved.

"As you all know," he said with a laugh, "my career as a rapper did not work out. But I decided to become something way cooler, an educator. I wanted to help kids become connected and engaged, just like Mr. Martin did for me."

Knowing firsthand that deeper relationships and support from adults in the school increase connectedness and engagement, Amari decided to build advisory periods into the weekly schedule. All faculty and staff members at Rockville are advisers, each serving the same small group of students from the time they enter ninth grade until they graduate. To facilitate this initiative, class periods were shortened by five minutes, which allowed for 30 minutes at the end of the day for advisory time. When they first envisioned this, Amari and the faculty considered the best possible use of those minutes, and they took inspiration from Google's 20% time (which allowed employees to dedicate 20% of their time to passion projects). They chose to devote the minutes to student-driven projects, stipulating that the projects must adhere to a few guidelines. First, they must offer an innovative solution to a community problem. Next, students must research and acquire knowledge about the issue. Third, students must involve community members or organizations in their solutions.

Innovation Day is an annual event and the culmination of the students' yearlong efforts, during which they present their projects. Their presentations include the issues they've been addressing, the solutions they've tried, and what they learned. This year, the theme for the event was Rethinking. The students were challenged with looking at an existing problem from a new perspective and reconsidering, redefining, and reevaluating the issue. The stakes were higher than previous years as several businesses in the community had collectively created a fund to offer the winning group a $5,000 grant to support their project. The teams would be presenting to a panel of eight judges from the community, and I was assigned to help the judges by distributing, collecting, and tabulating scoresheets. And so, with plenty of sharpened pencils and my favorite calculator, I pulled into the Rockville parking lot eager to see what happened as the day unfolded.

Rethinking Stress

I entered the auditorium and introduced myself to the judges. The five teams chosen as finalists were sitting behind them, and I offered each student some words of encouragement. These young people were models of grace under pressure. I knew they had been preparing their presentations for weeks, and even with that preparation, they were surely experiencing some anxiety. "How are you doing? Are you nervous?" I asked one young man.

"I'm just telling myself it's excitement," he smiled, one of his knees bouncing up and down and knocking the notebook off his lap.

His response fit perfectly with the theme of rethinking. Psychologists and researchers Jeremy Jamieson, Matthew Nock, and Wendy Mendes study the reframing of stress as challenge. According to these researchers, a stress response (rapid heartbeat and shallow breathing) is affected by certain situations but also by our *perception* of those situations. Our brains and bodies are connected, and when we perceive a situation as stressful, our bodies prepare for a threat. When we reframe the situation as a challenge, however, our bodies prepare for positive outcomes. There is a catch, though: In order to stave off a stress reaction, we must also appraise our available resources as sufficient to meet the challenge.

By practicing this reframing of stress as challenge, we can decrease the unhelpful emotional impact and develop more adaptive emotional and physiological responses to stress. Over time, changing the way we think about stress can positively impact our mental and physical well-being and can also improve our performance. When we frame a situation as a challenge rather than a threat, we are better able to identify opportunities. Elite athletes from football quarterbacks to baseball pitchers understand the importance of embracing challenge and appraising their resources as sufficient to meet each one. Their success depends on staying in a positive mental state and spotting opportunities amid the pressure. Our success depends upon our ability to do that, too. By thoroughly preparing for their presentations, the students were ready for a challenge and affirmed they had the necessary resources to succeed.

Understanding the power of reframing stress will serve these students well now and in the future.

Apples to Agape

After Amari made opening remarks, introduced the judges, and acknowledged dignitaries in the audience, he invited the first team to the stage. Their project was titled "Apples to Agape." The name alone piqued my interest because gape, Greek for brotherly love, is one of my favorite words. The students explained that a nearby apple farm had been discarding several piles of apples each week, and the students wondcred if these discarded apples might be useful for addressing food insecurity in the community. The farm was willing to give away their discarded or rejected apples (the ones with bruises or mushy spots), but the students soon discovered these apples aren't the best for snacking. Imperfect apples, however, are ideal for cooking. As the apples break down during cooking, the natural sugars concentrate, transforming them into something sweet and delicious. Imperfect apples can become the main ingredient for apple sauce, apple strudel, apple crisp, and apple pie, a perfect metaphor for the way something beautiful can come from a problem.

Now the students needed some willing and able bakers. Through determination and networking, the students found a group of ladies at a local church who love to bake, and a helpful church member with a pick-up truck. During apple harvesting season (July to November), they visited the farm every Wednesday and brought bags of apples back to the church. The ladies made all sorts of apple treats and even froze some for the colder months when apples aren't in season. The students then delivered their delectable creations to a local soup kitchen, as well as provided some for the church's meal delivery outreach to elderly neighbors in need. In their presentation, the students reflected on what they learned about farming, food preparation, and food insecurity in their community. They also shared what they learned about persistence and problem-solving.

Two more groups presented before intermission, and I had a chance to talk with the Apples to Agape team during the break. I asked what inspired their project, and Alisha, the leader of the group, told me she was inspired by Mrs. Cole, the second grade teacher who helped her develop a passion for service.

"I remember early in the school year, Mrs. Cole told us that we were going to adopt some grandparents at the senior center down the road," Alisha explained, finishing a cookie from the refreshment table. "I did feel a little wary the first time we visited. Many of the people were in wheelchairs, and some of them had trouble speaking. I didn't really know what to do or say." Alisha said that Mrs. Cole had directed each of the students to select a book to read to one of the seniors and practice reading it before their visit. "I could see how happy it made them when we read the stories and showed them the pictures. It was like the energy shifted in the room, and we brought them back to life."

Alisha admitted that she began to look forward to the monthly visits. "We made crafts with them around every holiday, and we continued to read stories. They were so excited when we arrived, and when we had to leave, they always asked when we were coming back." She paused for a moment before adding, "I guess that's when I realized how good it felt to help somebody else. I know we helped them, but I became a better person in the process."

I chatted with Alisha and her group about the benefits of service-learning and the satisfaction found in helping. We also talked about the challenges and obstacles that can get in the way of projects and initiatives. "It's definitely not all sunshine and roses," one of Alisha's teammates admitted. "There are logistical challenges and just finding the time. At first, we couldn't figure out how to get the apples from the farm to the church. Then, we couldn't figure out how to sustain the project when apple-picking season was over. The answers seem so simple now, but at the time, those problems really stumped us. Even though we sometimes had heated arguments, our adviser helped us focus on the task and make sure our arguments were productive."

The Power of Rethinking

My chat with Alisha's group (and the theme of the Innovation Day event itself) led me to recall the work of Adam Grant, organizational psychologist and author. In his book, *Think Again: The Power of Knowing What You Don't Know*, he extols the benefits of thinking like a scientist and reminds us to focus our conflict on tasks rather than relationships. According to Grant, when we are under stress, we tend to cling to familiar and automatic thoughts and behaviors. We rely on old assumptions, instincts, or habits, even when they are not helpful. A more useful approach is to think like a scientist: consider the evidence, hold any assumptions loosely, and test those assumptions out. Start with intellectual humility; know what you don't know. Question your knowledge in the face of new evidence, then become curious about the information you don't yet have. In a rapidly shifting world, it's important to be able to adapt and change rather than stubbornly holding onto old ideas and opinions.

Thinking like a scientist is helpful, but it's challenging, particularly when working on a team. Grant warns against being too agreeable in collaborative work. While agreeable people are lovely, a team full of agreeable people is unlikely to come up with innovative solutions. We must agree on the why, but disagreeing on the how can yield better outcomes. Disagreeing with an intent to elevate the work can be productive. However, the disagreement must be focused on the task rather than the relationships. Relationship-focused conflict is personal, emotional, and filled with friction, and it causes us to dig in our heels and resist rethinking. Task conflict, on the other hand, brings a diversity of thought to the table. It reveals things we don't know and allows us to be more flexible in our thinking.

Rubbish to Refuge

By the time I finished my conversation with Alisha's team, we were called back to our seats for the next presentation. The presentation immediately following intermission was titled Rubbish to Refuge. These students had identified the abundance of discarded items (often ending up by roadways or on curbs) as an issue they could address. Inspired by the school's art teacher, they decided to turn that trash into treasure by creating sculptures from the items they picked up. They partnered with the community center to plan an art show where their creations could be sold and their profits donated to the center. They also found opportunities to teach children in the center's after school program about the creative process. When they found a dozen discarded tires, they involved the kids in painting the planters they fashioned from them. During their presentation, I marveled at the photos of their pieces: a bird bath made from a discarded pedestal sink, a trellis made from an old piece of fencing, and a bookshelf that started as a rickety ladder. There was a wine glass holder made from a garden rake that made me jealous of the lucky patron who bought it. One student even created a captivating piece of wall art from pallet boards and bottle caps. I imagined the beauty these pieces brought to the yards and homes of community members.

It takes vision to see the potential in something discarded. These items have stories. They were once appreciated and used, but most people would have concluded they were no longer worth anything. The experience of looking for the beauty and possibility in something seemingly worthless would surely serve students well. It's pausing, pondering, and persisting in action. The students first had to push aside their assumptions about the usefulness and value of these objects. Then, they had to become open-minded and curious about the possibilities. And, they had to persist in figuring out how to bring their vision for the objects to life. It's exactly what their teachers and advisors were doing for them—appreciating the students just as they currently are but also holding a vision for what they can become. Looking past assumptions and seeing possibilities is both a mindset and a skill, and it can be cultivated with practice.

After all the groups had presented and the judges were completing their scoresheets, I had a few minutes to talk with Terrell, a member of the Rubbish to Refuge team. When I asked about the inspiration for the project, he told me about Mr. Rudd, his art teacher and adviser.

"Until Mr. Rudd came into my life, I didn't know how to deal with frustration," Terrell began. "As soon as something got hard or wasn't turning out the way I wanted, I just quit. But in art class, my teacher didn't let me quit." Terrell leaned back on the folded auditorium chair. "Mr. Rudd calls problems and mistakes 'happy accidents' and says some of the most interesting art comes from just going with the process."

Terrell shared his realization that he was getting in his own way. By quitting when things didn't go as expected, he was missing opportunities.

"I've learned that if I just adjust and keep going, the result is often even better than what I originally imagined. I'm so grateful that Mr. Rudd taught me a productive way to look at challenges and obstacles." I was in awe of Mr. Rudd's ability to teach this powerful life lesson in his art classroom, and I became determined to meet him before the day was over.

Rethinking Positive Thinking

Positive thinking is widely touted in education, but it doesn't always serve us well. Obstacles (like those Terrell encountered) are inevitable, and if we aren't prepared for them, we can get knocked off course. Psychologist and researcher Gabriele Oettingen proposes that we rethink positive thinking. Instead of only thinking positive thoughts when it comes to our future goals, we should actively identify the obstacles that could get in our way of achieving those goals. According to Oettingen, identifying and visualizing a dream fulfilled feels good, but that good feeling can lull us into complacency. Instead, we should practice mental contrasting, comparing where we are now to where we want to be. Then we can make a plan that includes both action steps and strategies for overcoming likely obstacles. Doing so gives us the motivation and energy to do what it takes to succeed.

Oettingen suggests we use an exercise called WOOP to make achieving our goals more likely. WOOP—an acronym for wish, outcome, obstacles, plans—begins by creating a wish, something that feels energizing, challenging, and feasible. Write down the wish in one phrase or sentence. Then, envision the outcome, identify and visualize the benefits of the wish being realized. Be as clear and specific as possible about what life would be like after the achievement. Next, focus on any obstacles that could get in the way, particularly those that are self-created or internal, such as a tendency to procrastinate or make unhelpful choices. After the obstacles are identified, create "if ... then" plans. For example, if I find myself watching reality TV rather than working on my goal, I will set my timer for 20 minutes and refocus. The final step is to take action on the plan you created. The WOOP process is easily applicable to almost any goal, and Oettingen suggests going through the steps daily to keep the goal (and the plan) front of mind. While being blindly optimistic feels good, being blind to potential obstacles is often a path to frustration and failure.

A Room Full of Winners

When the judges finished with their scoresheets, I collected, tabulated, and recorded the total scores for each group on a summary document. I then handed the stack to Amari, and he conferred with the award committee. To my surprise, Amari made an announcement that the committee needed a few extra minutes before announcing the winner. That seems odd, I thought. There wasn't a tie in the total scores. As it turned out, only a point separated the top two groups.

I decided to use the wait time to look for Mr. Rudd, whom I found right outside the auditorium doors. I introduced myself, happily sharing what his students had said and affirming that he was making a lasting impact. A sweet combination of emotions overtook him for a moment, and he smiled while wiping away a tear.

"As a teacher, it's so hard to know that you are making a difference," he confessed. "I try to get to know my students in order to understand both their strengths and their challenges. That way I can build on their strengths and help them overcome what is holding them back." We talked about the project his advisory group had presented, and I commented that he must be very proud. "The students really did all the work. I just made suggestions and provided feedback," he replied. Just as his students had lovingly brought out the beauty in their found objects, he brought out what was special about each of them. By the time we finished our conversation, Amari was calling all attendees back to their seats.

"We are ready to announce the winners," he began. "Yes, I said *winners*. Our generous community sponsors have agreed to award the top two teams with a $5,000 grant." Applause and cheers erupted, and Amari had to wait for the room to quiet again. "The first grant winner is … Rubbish to Refuge!" Mr. Rudd and his students jumped out of their seats, and practically tumbled in a big, hugging heap onto the stage. They received a large cardboard check and posed for a picture. Then the audience grew quiet again.

"Before I announce the second winner," Amari said, "I want you to know how proud I am of all of you, both students and advisers. It takes hard work, great thought, and commitment to create innovative solutions to stubborn problems. I have no doubt that after you leave Rockville, you will go out and change the world." The audience clapped, and a few shouted pleas for him to get on with it.

"And now, the second winner is … Apples to Agape!" Alisha and her team hugged and cried and hugged some more before finally making their way onto the stage. Although I had no role in helping these teams, I was beaming with pride, too. I felt so proud of Amari, my student who was now teaching me so much about leadership. And standing in the auditorium at the end of this exciting day, I felt especially proud to be an educator.

Rethinking Teaching and Leading

On the drive home, I reflected on how easy it is to let our roles determine how we act and interact in a school, but what if we reconsidered the importance of titles and roles? If leadership is about influence, then teachers are surely leaders, and students can be leaders, too. After all, the best policies are crafted with teachers and students at the table. Each brings a unique perspective to decision-making in a school. While rethinking widely accepted roles and norms, Rockville's successful Innovation Day had also affirmed my belief that education could benefit from more experimentation with new and innovative practices.

By this point in the book, you know that my mind tends to wander while I'm driving. On this particular trip home, it wandered to the movie *The King's Speech*. In this historical flick, England's Prince Albert (played by Colin Firth) is about to ascend the throne after the death of his father and the scandalous abdication of King Edward VIII. But there's just one problem: He has a debilitating speech impediment. With England on the brink of war, a commanding and confident leader is imperative. So, after many failed attempts at correcting his speech, Albert's wife hires a speech therapist with unorthodox methods. It's an inspiring tale which highlights both the courage to take a different approach and the power of a teacher. Lionel (Albert's speech therapist) has a background in theater and uses that to rethink treatment. And in the process, Albert begins to rethink what it means to be a real leader.

The ability to unlearn is as essential as the ability to learn. Rethinking compels us to consider what is no longer serving us and let it go. Once we shed old assumptions and practices, we can open ourselves up to new possibilities. There is always pressure to stick with the status quo, but that's not the best way to navigate a rapidly changing world. It's far more energizing and impactful to try something new. From using discarded apples to feed the hungry to making sculptures from salvaged finds, Rockville's students artfully embraced rethinking. Soon I would be heading to Hilldale High School to meet with another group of students focused on the future. The school district uses an innovative approach designed to attract talented young people to the teaching profession. I was excited to talk with Hilldale's aspiring teachers about their introduction to teaching.

 ## Leveraging the Power of Rethinking

Pausing and Rethinking
Stressful situations can tempt you to fall into familiar and automatic thoughts and behaviors. You may find yourself relying on old assumptions, instincts, or habits, even when they're not helpful. Instead of going into automatic pilot, pause and take a

breath. Try thinking like a scientist, give yourself space to check your assumptions and test new approaches.

Pondering and Rethinking

A stress response (rapid heartbeat and shallow breathing) is affected by certain situations but also by your *perception* of the situation. Your brain and body are connected, and when you perceive a situation as stressful, your body prepares for a threat. By reframing the situation as a challenge instead, your body prepares for positive outcomes. Ask yourself, *What is the opportunity in this challenge? How could pursuing it improve my life or the lives of others?* Instead of stressing about what could go wrong, allow yourself to imagine what could go right.

Persisting and Rethinking

Positive thinking doesn't always serve you well. Obstacles are inevitable, and if you aren't prepared for them, they can throw you off course. Instead of just thinking positive thoughts, actively identify the obstacles that could get in your way. Practice mental contrasting, comparing where you are now to where you want to be. Then make a plan that includes both action steps and strategies for overcoming likely obstacles. Staying positive and having a concrete plan for the inevitable bumps in the road helps you persist.

 Questions for Reflection

What are your automatic thoughts and behaviors in stressful situations? How might reframing those stressful situations as challenges help you choose more helpful thoughts and behaviors?

What issues and problems recurrently impact your work? How can you rethink those problems to find new and creative solutions?

How can you work more effectively with colleagues and students to find innovative solutions to recurring problems?

Notes and Works Cited

Jamieson, J. P., Nock, M. K., & Mendes, W. B. (2012). Mind over matter: Reappraising arousal improves cardiovascular and cognitive responses to stress. *Journal of Experimental Psychology*, *141*(3), 417–422.

Grant, A. (2021). *Think again: The power of knowing what you don't know*. Viking.

Oettingen, G. (2014). *Rethinking positive thinking: Inside the new science of motivation*. Current.

Clark, N. (2017). *The positive journal: 5 minutes a day toward a happier life*. Union Square & Co.

Hooper, T., Canning, I., Sherman, E., Unwin, G., Seidler, D., Firth, C., Rush, G., Bonham Carter, H., Pearce, G., Spall, T., Jacobi, D., Ehle, J., Andrews, A., Bloom, C., Best, E., Gambon, M., Desplat, A., & Cohen, D. (2011). *The king's speech*. UK Film Council.

10

The Power of Purpose

I filled my travel mug with tea and packed a bag of trail mix before heading down the mountain to visit the Aspiring Educator class at Hilldale High School. This elective class is part of a teacher recruiting initiative in the school district. It began when leaders realized the best way to attract great teachers to the district may be to grow their own. Students can self-select into the class, but often, teachers identify students who demonstrate characteristics associated with great teaching, such as collaboration, adaptability, empathy, and patience. The instructor for Hilldale's aspiring teachers is Leslie Fabin, a math teacher with 15 years of experience. I'd talked with Leslie several times before my visit, and she often conveyed the challenge of nurturing her students' enthusiasm while being honest about the challenges of teaching.

Hilldale's aspiring teachers meet for class right after lunch, and on days they do not meet together, they get to observe teaching across their district in a variety of grade levels and subjects. Hilldale is a small, rural district, with little mobility. Therefore, the students often have the opportunity to observe in the classrooms of their former teachers. I couldn't wait to hear their reflections on seeing their old classrooms from a new perspective. My visit was scheduled on a class meeting day, and I'd been asked to speak to the group about the ways teachers make a lasting impact on students' lives. They'd been reading *Safe, Seen, and Stretched in the Classroom*, and they had questions.

DOI: 10.4324/9781003344735-11

I began with an overview of the book's content and high-lighted some of the stories illustrating teacher impact, then opened the floor to the students. They first inquired about why some teachers seem so passionate about teaching while others seem to just be going through the motions. Diving into this question, we talked about the importance of finding meaning and purpose in the work we do. When our work begins to feel meaningless, it's easy to slip into a pattern of indifference or apathy.

Cierra (whose book was tabbed and highlighted) drew our attention to Chapter 4, the section in which I wrote about a conversation with Rafael, one of my graduate students. We'd been talking about impactful teachers, and Rafael described the difference between teaching focused on connection and teaching that felt more transactional. Rafael was distinguishing between the high school teachers he remembered clearly and those who were less memorable. In the more memorable classes, he remembered specific things about the classroom and could recall the distinctive words and actions of the teacher. Those were the classrooms where he felt a connection with the teacher and a sense of belonging in the classroom community. In the less memorable classrooms, relationships seemed transactional. The teacher assigned the work, the students completed it, and the teacher graded it. According to Rafael, most of those teachers were kind enough, but they didn't make an impact on his life. It was as if they were just fulfilling some unspoken agreement in order to get through the class period without incident.

The difference between transactional teaching and teaching for connection resonated with the aspiring teachers (still high school students themselves), and they provided additional examples. One student offered an observation, in classrooms where students and teachers are connected, there are inside jokes, things only the class and the teacher understand. Another student commented that people know each other in a connected classroom, but in a transactional classroom they may not even know each other's names. We talked about evidence of connection, and a student proposed laughter as one telltale sign. In transactional classrooms, laughter is rare, but we all agreed that laughing together can be a sign of a connected and engaged classroom community. The students also added that teaching centered on connection is characterized by flexibility and responsiveness to student needs. They felt more connected to teachers who made an effort to understand them as people and as learners.

Work that Matters

Giving some final thoughts on connection and answering the remaining student questions, I shifted to posing my own questions to the group. "Why are you considering a career in teaching?" I began. Brodie raised his hand first. "I want to support kids who feel like giving up and show them there is a better future ahead." I wondered out loud if a teacher had modeled that for him.

"Definitely," Brodie said, leaning forward on his desk. "Mr. Tanner was my middle school science teacher, and he helped me see that I could make a contribution to the world, that my life mattered. I felt so lost in seventh grade. My mom was going through a rough time, and I went to live with my aunt. She was nice to me, but she was busy with her own life. I began to run around with a bunch of kids making poor choices because they made me feel accepted and included." Brodie described a time he got caught skipping class and was picked up on the corner by the school resource officer. Luckily, he was returned to Mr. Tanner's classroom.

"Most adults had written me off, given up on me. But Mr. Tanner talked to me like a real person," Brodie continued. "He asked me about my dreams for the future. I didn't really have any, so he asked me about what I liked to do. I told him I liked playing soccer, but I had to quit when I moved in with my aunt." Brodie's teacher told him that he recently volunteered to coach his young son's soccer team and was trying to learn more about the game. He invited Brodie to help.

"I went with Mr. Tanner to the team's soccer practices after school, and he kept reminding me that I was a role model for the young players." Brodie revealed how he took that seriously and tried to demonstrate the importance of sportsmanship and teamwork as well as the soccer fundamentals. "I'll never forget the day Mr. Tanner gave me a team jersey with Assistant Coach on the back. Working with the kids made me feel important, like my effort mattered. I think teaching will make me feel the same way." The other students echoed Brodie's sentiment. They wanted to pursue work that felt meaningful, work that made a difference.

Job, Career, or Calling

The students' comments led me to share some research from organizational psychologist Amy Wrzesniewski, who distinguishes a job or career from a calling. People who view their work with a job orientation see it as a means to an end. The work provides the financial resources needed to support themselves and their families, and they prefer that it does not interfere with their personal lives. For people who view their work as a job, working is a necessity, but it doesn't provide a sense of identity or meaning. They may cultivate hobbies or other interests to bring purpose or meaning into their lives.

Those with a career orientation are more likely to focus on success or prestige. They seek upward mobility, promotions, and titles, and so, a role with opportunities for advancement suits their career aspirations. A calling, on the other hand, brings a sense of identity and fulfillment. Like these aspiring teachers, those with a calling orientation seek work that contributes to the greater good and makes the world a better place. Although a higher salary is always desirable, a calling brings fulfillment from the work itself. According to Wrzesniewski, people with a calling orientation typically derive a greater sense of satisfaction from their work.

It's difficult to predict a person's orientation toward work based on their job description or salary. Almost any role can be enacted as a job, career, or calling, depending on how the work is framed. People often select professional roles based on their values, and if service is valued, they are more likely to seek work they deem impactful. Those searching for a calling are likely to choose a vocation like teaching because of the opportunity to make a difference. Teachers often cite helping students evolve and grow as the most meaningful part of their work. Supporting colleagues through difficult times also provides a sense of meaning, especially when mentoring new teachers. These students already knew that supporting others creates ripples of impact in the world. They knew it because they had seen it modeled by their teachers.

Leslie's efforts to temper her students' idealism with a dose of realism were justified. Because teaching matters so very much, teachers at times feel depleted and defeated. Every teacher experiences seasons of struggle, especially when there is incongruence between the tasks they find most meaningful and the tasks which take up much of their days. When teachers feel pressured to stick to a crowded curriculum map or are burdened by an overabundance of paperwork, they have less time to focus on the parts of their work that bring fulfillment, and, it goes without saying, create the most impact. When a calling starts to lose its meaning, Wrzesniewski suggests strategies for recrafting the role.

Job-crafting is about redesigning what we do at work: reconsidering tasks, relationships, and perceptions. According to Wrzesniewski, we can find more meaning in the same role by changing what we do and how we think about what we do. We craft ourselves a job that (while still meeting the obligations and requirements) is more aligned with our strengths, motives, and passions. Task-crafting involves adding or dropping tasks and responsibilities to better align with individual talents. For example, a teacher who has a gift for art may be able to drop bus duty in exchange for overseeing the after-school art club.

Relationship-crafting concerns reshaping the type and nature of the interactions we have with others, which may require a closer look at how we spend our time. We may decide to change our classroom routines to allow more time for one-on-one discussions with students in order to add more meaningful interaction to our days.

Task-crafting and relationship-crafting are strategies for increasing what lights us up and decreasing what burns us out. But sometimes our assigned tasks and schedules are outside of our control. Rather than changing our routines or to-do lists, cognitive crafting involves changing our mindsets about the things we do. By changing perspectives, we can find or create more meaning in what might otherwise be seen as busy work. For example, grading papers can be viewed as a mundane task or an opportunity to give valuable feedback and show students they are worthy of our time and effort. Bus duty can be seen as a delay in getting to important work or as the vital task of ensuring that each student gets to and from school safely. Cognitive crafting empowers us to find more meaning in the work we do. Through reconsidering tasks, relationships, and mindsets, we can get more satisfaction out of our days. Leslie and I both knew these aspiring teachers would hit some bleak points in their professional lives, and we wanted them to be prepared.

Work and Life Satisfaction

After Brodie finished telling us about his call to teach and we talked about our work as a calling, Delia volunteered. She didn't have a turning point with a teacher that led her to this career path, but she carried a collage of memories from her favorite teachers' classrooms. "I just remember feeling happy in those classrooms, and I want to feel that sense of joy in my work," she confessed. When I asked her for an example, she told us about her third-grade teacher, Mrs. Prevatt.

"Her classroom was always colorful and inviting, but she changed it up all the time," Delia began. "In the fall, Mrs. Prevatt brought in pumpkins and leaves, and the bookshelf was filled with spooky stories. In the spring, she brought in caterpillars and flowers. And it wasn't unusual for our teacher to show up in a costume or with props to go along with the things we were studying. I still remember her arriving dressed like Martha Washington in February when we were learning about the Presidents of the United States."

Delia described Mrs. Prevatt's classroom in such detail that I could picture it in my mind, and her exuberant hand gestures conveyed her enthusiasm. "Even as a young child, I knew I wanted to do that, to wear the costumes, and sing the songs, and bring the outside world in. I can't imagine myself sitting at a desk or working in an office," she said. "I know teachers don't get paid as much, but I need to do work that makes me happy."

The other students affirmed Delia's quest for happiness, but they also seemed to understand the economics related to their career choice. Leslie had shared the district's teacher salary scale with them, and they'd discussed the impact of income on their future lifestyle choices. They could see that their starting salary would be fairly aligned with the starting pay in other professions requiring similar levels of education and credentials. But as they spent more years in teaching, the salary gap between them and other professionals would widen. Although finding joy and meaning in work is important, the stress of financial burdens can have a negative impact on well-being. Leslie and I wanted them to understand the trade-offs teachers must consider.

Flourishing as a Teacher

While Delia isn't alone in her pursuit of happiness, happiness can be difficult to define. Martin Seligman (often called the "father of positive psychology") has focused his work more specifically on flourishing, finding fulfillment in our lives, pursuing meaningful and worthwhile endeavors, and connecting with others at a deeper level. Traditionally, psychology has attended to the relieving of human suffering and treating disorders. But Seligman proposed that relieving suffering is not enough. People want to flourish, and the skills that build flourishing are different from the skills that alleviate suffering.

Seligman identified five components of flourishing: positive emotion, engagement, relationships, meaning, and accomplishment (PERMA). Our tendency to experience positive emotions can vary with temperament and circumstances, but within limits, we can increase good feelings. We can cultivate gratitude and forgiveness to find more peace and contentment in remembering the past. We can embrace the present by savoring pleasures and practicing mindfulness. And we can feel better about the future by building hope in the form of goals and dreams. And as we immerse ourselves in work that fully deploys our skills, strengths, and attention, our engagement in that work can bring satisfaction and bliss.

Relationships are fundamental to our well-being, and the other components of flourishing are often amplified through them. We are likely to experience more positive emotions, such as joy and belonging with others, and when we are engaged in collaboration with others, we can experience a collective sense of accomplishment. Strong relationships can give our lives meaning, and supportive relationships are beneficial in navigating difficult times. A sense of purpose can be derived from serving others or being in service to something bigger than the self. Helping others could very well be one of the best things we can do for ourselves.

Satisfaction at work and satisfaction in life are strongly correlated. Delia somehow understood that choosing a career path based on happiness could lead to a more fulfilling life. Loving our work helps us love our lives, and being happy in our lives certainly spills over into our work. It is difficult to flourish if we spend over half of our waking hours doing work that doesn't feel meaningful. Although there are many influences on our happiness, our attitudes and actions play a significant part. Crafting meaningful, satisfying work is much about our choices, how we view our tasks and nurture our relationships. It takes practice and commitment to sustain our well-being and happiness at work, but it also takes support from leaders in the school and broader organization. The benefits of attending to teacher well-being and flourishing within the organization include enhanced individual and organizational learning, improved performance, less absenteeism, and decreased susceptibility to burnout. After all, teacher well-being is essential to achieving better student outcomes. What's good for teachers is good for kids.

Do What You Love

After Delia shared, several more students revealed their reasons for choosing teaching and the role models who inspired them. Then Chris, a quiet student seated in the back of the room, turned to Leslie and asked why she became a teacher. I moved aside and gave her the floor.

"The younger me gave in to pressure from my parents to choose a career that fit their definition of success," she began. "So, I double majored in economics and finance and got a job at a financial services firm. I spent all day in an office working on reports, and I hated it."

Leslie was open about the impact on her mental health. She talked about going to a counselor who asked her to remember a time when she did something that made her feel happy. "It didn't take me long to realize it was math class," she said. "I know it sounds strange, but math makes me happy. I was always fascinated by the patterns, and I loved the satisfaction of working on a problem until I got the right answer."

Leslie scooted up onto the stool at the front of the classroom and began to describe her high school math teacher. "Mrs. Keyes got as excited as I did when I solved a problem. Getting a high five from her was always the highlight of my day. She made math engaging and fun. When I remembered Mrs. Keyes in that counselor's office, I knew what I needed to do."

Leslie told the students how she went back to school to get a teaching degree. "The days I spent in a corporate office felt lonely and gray, but I feel alive every day in this classroom. Teaching isn't for everyone, but you can't deny it when it calls you."

Just as Leslie finished telling her story, the bell rang. I said my goodbyes to the aspiring teachers. Then I watched as Leslie high-fived every student going out the door.

Flourishing or Languishing

With the students gone, Leslie and I had a few minutes to talk. We shared a mutual concern for our profession: too many teachers leaving and not enough coming in to fill the vacancies. An exodus of experienced, effective teachers leaves a mighty void. Instead of flourishing, more and more teachers were languishing. Feeling listless and aimless, languishing is like looking at life through a dirty window. It's characterized by a lack of motivation and fatigue. The important tasks still get done, but we don't have our usual energy. The term languishing was popularized by organizational psychologist Adam Grant, who wanted to name the emotion so many were feeling as the pandemic entered its second year. His article on feeling blah was the most-read New York Times story of 2021. But even as we emerge from the pandemic fog, many teachers are still experiencing the blahs. According to Grant, this emotion is particularly sinister because, over time, we may not even notice the dulling of our delight or the dwindling of our drive. When we don't realize we are suffering, we don't seek support or strategies.

Languishing is the absence of well-being, and certainly not the path to flourishing. Grant suggests that attending to the PERMA components of flourishing could help pull us out of these feelings of stagnation and bleakness. Engaging in meaningful tasks and projects may be the best antidote to languishing, and doing these tasks with others can stave off feelings of isolation. Teaching is a profession that lends itself to connection and meaning-making, if we can reduce the barriers that get in the way. Packing curriculum calendars, over-scheduling, and piling on paperwork make it difficult to sift through the mundane to focus on the meaningful. It's up to all of us to advocate for the removal of barriers to teacher well-being.

Educational settings are also often rife with unhelpful positive phrases. We encourage each other to look on the bright side or to choose joy. Instead of looking on the bright side, what if we looked on the meaningful side? What if we found significance in the difficulties? When the inevitable challenges come, we can frame them as opportunities to be leveraged rather than problems to avoid. Tough situations can be transformed into occasions for growth, development, and impact. Brodie's difficulties became the catalyst for a turning point in his life, thanks to Mr. Tanner. And Leslie's depression became the doorway to a life she loves. The light is always there behind the dirty window of languishing, but we may need support and strategies to find it. Visiting Leslie and her aspiring teachers had energized me and reaffirmed the meaning in teaching.

A Life Spent Teaching

Thinking about the meaning of a life spent teaching always brings to mind Richard Dreyfuss's portrayal of Glenn Holland in the movie, *Mr. Holland's Opus*. Glenn Holland is a composer who decides to take a teaching job to support his family. In his mind, it's a temporary position, and it leaves him free in the evenings to focus on composing his symphony, which he believes will be his legacy. Noticing the lack of student engagement in his classes, the principal challenges him to do better, to inspire a love of music in his students and teach meaningful lessons. He finds many challenges that become opportunities to impact students' lives, from an anxious clarinet player to a rhythm-deficient athlete who needs a music credit. Through the years, his job turns into his calling.

Years turn into decades, and Glenn Holland realizes he never brought his symphony to life. Pushed into retirement after budget cuts, he finally gets an opportunity to lead the student orchestra in the opus he's been composing. As the music progresses, the orchestra seats are filled by former students returning to express their gratitude, and as each one is seated, Mr. Holland comes to rcalize that his true legacy resides in the lives of his students he impacted.

As an educator, I've watched this film more times than I can count. I'm always fascinated by Mr. Holland's transformation from apathetic temporary teacher to passionate and committed professional. It's a change in the way he views his role that brings purpose and meaning to his work and his life. But it's not without challenges, from work–life balance to boundaries, he's constantly pushed to grow. He's learning alongside his students about how to create the composition that becomes his life. While we may never hear our students play a symphony we composed, we can find satisfaction in knowing that we've left a legacy of impact. Teaching matters. *Teachers* matter.

 ## Leveraging the Power of Purpose

Pausing with Purpose

When we get into a pattern of constant busyness, we can easily wander into a funk or find ourselves languishing. We may think that pushing through is the solution, but often, the best antidote to impending burnout is a pause. A pause gives us time to check in with ourselves and assess our well-being. A pause also allows us to do some deeper evaluation. Rather than robotically checking things off a list, pausing gives us a chance to think more critically about our actions and interactions. In the midst of a pause, we can get back in touch with our purpose.

Pondering with Purpose

When we've lost a sense of meaning in our work, pondering can help us find it again. A time and task audit is a great place to start. Tracking how we spend our time can reveal helpful or unhelpful patterns. Ask yourself, *How often am I doing things that energize me or light me up? Are my days filled with tasks that feel meaningless? How can I shift that balance?* It can also be helpful to identify a personal mission and intentionally find ways to align daily tasks with that mission.

Persisting with Purpose

Purposeful persistence requires deciding in advance to stay on a course despite the inevitable challenges. We choose a purpose for our lives that feels important, and important paths aren't typically easy. Reframing is a helpful strategy for persisting through frustration and difficulties. Reframing challenges as opportunities to develop ourselves and impact others can help us find meaning in the struggles. After all, it's easier to stay on the path when we know why we are putting forth the effort.

 ## Questions for Reflection

What do you find most meaningful about your work? How can you bring that sense of meaning to your daily actions and interactions?

When do you find yourself losing your sense of purpose and just going through the motions? When that happens, how can you reconnect with your purpose?

What evidence can you find of your impact? How can you use that evidence to keep going during the difficult times?

Notes and Works Cited

Hasson, J. (2022). *Safe, seen, and stretched in the classroom: The remarkable ways teachers shape students' lives.* Routledge.

Wrzesniewski, A. (1999). *Jobs, careers, and callings: Work orientation and job transitions.* University of Michigan.

Seligman, M. E. P. (2011). *Flourish: A visionary new understanding of happiness and well-being.* Free Press.

Grant, A. (2021). There's a name for the blah you're feeling: It's called languishing. *The New York Times*, 19 April.

11

Putting It All Together

The week following my visit with the aspiring teachers at Hilldale High School was fall break at Appalachian State, so I had my
pick of classrooms as I searched for a space to spread out and do
some analysis on my data. The hallways, usually buzzing with
activity, were so eerily quiet that I could hear the hum of the flu-
orescent lights. Armed with Post-its and whiteboard markers, I
chose the classroom closest to my office and arranged my notes.
I began as I always do, by drawing a big circle in the middle of
the board. Inside the circle, I wrote my main research question:
How do teachers turn challenges into opportunities for impact?
Webbing out from the circle, I added data gathered from stories,
conversations, and observations, then grouped the data according to the components of the emerging framework: pausing,
pondering, and persisting.

Pausing

I'd been reflecting on a story recently shared with me at a fund-
raising dinner that supported the importance of a pause. I happened to be seated next to Daryl, the owner of a local restaurant,
and as dinner companions often do, we talked about our work.
I told him about my research, and he was interested in the idea
of pausing.

DOI: 10.4324/9781003344735-12

"In the food service business, it's easy to get irritated with a customer and react in frustration," he confessed. "We tell our servers to walk away for a moment and take a breath. Sometimes they need to tag another server to go over to the table, but I suppose teachers don't have anyone to tag when they're out of patience." Daryl and I talked about the fast pace and constant demands of teaching, and then to my surprise, he admitted being the source of his teachers' irritation in his younger years.

"I was not a strong student, and I had a whole host of strategies for getting out of work. At times, I resorted to pushing my teachers' buttons in hopes they would send me out of class," he began. "But I underestimated Mr. Webb, my high school social studies teacher."

Daryl recalled his teacher assigning a scavenger hunt using the Constitution of the United States. "It seemed overwhelming to me, and I blurted out, 'This is stupid!' I was ready to be kicked out, but Mr. Webb didn't even get upset." Daryl described the way his teacher used the outburst to talk about Freedom of Speech, and then he offered to give Daryl an alternate assignment: writing an essay on why kids don't need to learn about the Constitution. "Honestly, I couldn't think of any reasons and didn't want to write an essay. I ended up working on the scavenger hunt. And even though I had been a jerk, Mr. Webb helped me."

Daryl told me that Mr. Webb became his model of self-control, one that has served him well in the restaurant business. And because Daryl shared his story with me, Mr. Webb has become my example of the power of pausing. When someone does or says something that pushes a button or strikes a nerve, it is tempting to react in kind, but a hasty reaction can make the situation worse. Mr. Webb could have demeaned Daryl or sent him out of class, but that would have interrupted the whole classroom community. Daryl would not have been engaged in learning, and the education of other students could have been negatively impacted as well. And the inevitable regret that follows words spoken in anger could have wrecked the rest of the teacher's day. By taking a pause, Mr. Webb turned a challenging situation into an opportunity. He made a lasting impact on Daryl's life by modeling restraint, and in doing so, interrupted Daryl's pattern of work avoidance. He even found an opportunity to capitalize on a teachable moment about Freedom of Speech.

Practicing the Pause

It's natural to feel angry when a disrespectful remark or action interrupts a lesson. Charles Spielberger is a psychologist who specializes in the study of anger, which he defines as an emotional state that varies in intensity from mild irritation to intense fury and rage. According to Spielberger, we use a variety of both conscious and unconscious processes to deal with angry feelings. The three main approaches are expressing, suppressing, and calming. Expressing our anger in an assertive (not aggressive) way can be helpful, but we may not be able to do so effectively when emotions are strong. Suppressing our anger happens when we hold it in, stop thinking about it, and focus on something else. But over time, anger that is consistently turned inward may cause physical or mental health issues. The best approach in the moment may be a calming strategy. This entails not just controlling your outward behavior, but also taking steps to lower your heart rate, calm yourself down, and let the strong feelings subside.

In addition to deep breaths, a calming phrase can help ease intense emotions. Simply repeating something like *I choose peace* while taking deep breaths can help you return to a more centered and empowered state. My former colleague, Lori Keating, used to repeat *I am loving, patient, and kind*, while patting her hand over her heart. (On one particularly chaotic day in her kindergarten classroom, she was certain her chest would be bruised from all the patting.) And many of us remember Frank Costanza (the iconic character from the television show "Seinfeld") repeating *Serenity now* in an effort to keep his blood pressure lower. Not the best model, as he ended up red faced and screaming, "SERENITY NOW!" by the end of the show. Although Frank's demonstration of the calming phrase isn't helpful, humor is also a great calming tool.

I added a note about Mr. Webb to the whiteboard and high-lighted some of the other stories which provided evidence of the power of a pause. I pulled out the story of Mrs. Berns pushing past her annoyance with a scattered Shelby. When Shelby's missing papers and books posed a challenge, her teacher turned it into an opportunity to provide a sense of calm in a child's chaotic life. I also located my notes about Laura curbing her frustration over Marisol's lack of participation in a reader's theater lesson. When Marisol's refusal to participate threatened to disrupt the lesson, Laura leveraged that event into an opportunity to provide a listening ear and a sense of psychological safety. In each of those stories, the pause was the key to preserving peace, assessing situations more objectively, and putting teachers on the path to making an impact. Speaking or acting in haste can exacerbate a problem or damage a relationship. The pause is the safeguard that allows us to choose the most helpful response. It's important to remember the situation itself doesn't cause a reaction, but rather our interpretation, the story we create. Pausing applies the brakes so we can slow down and question that story. It allows us to check our assumptions and hold our stories up against the facts. Pausing allows us to stop and ponder.

Pondering

Searching my stack of stories for evidence of pondering, I pulled out a recent one, shared with me at a writing retreat. I was seated next to Monique, or Mo, as she preferred to be called. A writing teacher at a community college, her passion for education was unmistakable. Hearing about my research on how teachers turn challenges into opportunities, she wanted to add to my data with her story about Mrs. Choe.

"Until second grade, I don't think I ever spoke a word in school," she began. "My brother was killed in an accident when I was 4, and I felt anxious and uneasy anywhere but home. I could talk to my parents, but I just couldn't speak to anyone at school." Mo said that teachers and school staff often got frustrated with her. "They didn't know what to do with me, so most of the time, they just ignored me. But Mrs. Choe was different."

Mo remembered Mrs. Choe's curiosity and tenacity. "I think she viewed me as a puzzle, a mystery she was determined to solve. She gave me a small, erasable whiteboard so that I could communicate with her. When the other kids were busy working, she would come beside me to ask a question about what we were learning, and I would write a response." Mo took a sip of her coffee. "I remember sitting on the bench next to Mrs. Choe one day at recess. I brought my whiteboard out and we had a whole conversation about my dog, with her asking questions, and me writing responses. It became a regular thing for us, and I never felt pressured." Mo knew that her teacher often spoke with her mother and her pediatrician, seemingly looking for new ways to offer more support.

"By the end of the year, I began to speak to Mrs. Choe, and I would talk one-on-one with a few other kids. That classroom felt like a safe space to try. I found my voice there, and now I use my voice every day to teach my own students."

The Power of Curiosity

I loved the way Mo described Mrs. Choe's view of her struggle as a puzzle or a mystery. She clearly framed it as a challenge, and in grappling with that challenge, impacted Mo's life and facilitated her own growth. Todd Kashdan is a psychologist who specializes in the connection between well-being and performance (particularly in times of struggle). According to Kashdan, many of the coping mechanisms we use to reduce stress when dealing with a problem ultimately decrease the quality of our performance over time. Instead, the optimal tool for stressful situations may be curiosity. It brings us to a challenge with fresh eyes, to look at a problem like a scientist, full of questions and wonder. A curious stance primes our brains for learning, creativity, and problem-solving. And curiosity can help us break out of old habits to create new, more helpful patterns.

In addition to getting curious about our students, we can benefit from cultivating curiosity about ourselves. Kashdan suggests periodically asking the following questions: What is feeding my energy? What is draining me? What is helping me stay calm and focused amid the pressures?

Do I need to make any adjustments or changes? By asking ourselves these questions with genuine curiosity, we can become better teachers—and more resilient people.

Persisting

Thinking about curiosity and resilience led me to consider the data I had gathered around persistence. During my visit to Briarwood Elementary School, Naomi Jenkins modeled persistence with Thomas as she searched for strategies to help him learn to regulate his emotions. When I visited Troy at Heritage Middle School, he shared the story of Mrs. Baker's ongoing support throughout his struggles in foster care. And the teachers at Rockville High School persisted in their efforts to help students feel connected and engaged through advisory periods and innovative projects. In each of these cases, challenges were turned into opportunities for impact through ongoing effort and commitment. I'd added another new story to the data, which furthered my understanding of persistence. The story was shared by Jessinia, one of my own graduate students. During a class discussion about teaching diverse learners, she told her classmates and me about Ms. Carter.

"When I got my schedule on the first day of tenth grade, I noticed that my second period class was Biology with a new teacher named Carter," Jessinia began. "I walked into class expecting to see Mr. Carter, but I was surprised to be greeted at the door by Ms. Carter, a young woman of color." Jessinia talked about the ways her teacher challenged students' beliefs and biases in addition to teaching the science content. "Soon after the bell rang on that first day, Ms. Carter passed out blank sheets of paper and asked us to draw a scientist. Most of us drew older men with crazy hair and glasses, like Einstein." Jessinia remembered her surprise when Ms. Carter followed that exercise with a series of slides showing acclaimed scientists of many different racial, ethnic, and gender identities.

"My mind was blown. As a young woman of color myself, I had never even considered a career in the sciences." Jessinia told us how Ms. Carter continued to plan activities that challenged students' limiting beliefs. "Even when I wanted to take the easy way out, she never gave up on me. Ms. Carter became an important mentor and advocate. She helped me get into college, and now I'm working on my doctorate. I try to pay it forward by encouraging other young women to consider paths they never believed were possible."

As a young teacher, Ms. Carter must have experienced some difficulties in learning to teach the content and her students. It's tempting to think that having talent or excellent training is the key to great teaching, but even the most solid foundational skills won't take us far without persistence. It is through trial and error, reflection, and skill-building that teachers learn to adapt their teaching for a diverse group of students with a variety of needs. What works with one student or one class may not work with others. Persistence is the key to becoming an effective teacher and continuing to grow.

Thinking about Mo's story and the other stories I'd laid across the tables, I was struck by how interrelated the components of the framework are. In classrooms where teachers feel satisfaction in teaching and make a positive impact on students' lives, the practices of pausing, pondering, and persisting were evident. First, teachers paused before reacting to an unexpected challenge, which allowed them to intentionally choose a response rather than being driven by circumstances or their own emotions. Next, they suspended assumptions and approached the challenge from a place of curiosity. This pondering allowed them to more fully understand their students' needs and determine a course of action. Finally, they persisted in this dance of patient inquiry and thoughtful responses in a way that led to better outcomes. Pausing and pondering helped them identify the best response to a challenge, but it took persistence to consistently employ those practices. And persisting required getting quiet and curious in order to keep taking the next right step.

The Head and the Heart

It felt strange to have this uninterrupted quiet time to think deeply about the data and what it all meant. It was in itself a pause—a respite from my busy life, typically full of competing priorities and interruptions—and a chance to ponder. I'd intentionally left my phone in my car and put an automatic "out of office" response on my email, but I felt a bit anxious and lost, as if experiencing withdrawal from constant connectivity and distraction. Intuition is an important tool in data analysis, and it's almost impossible to access intuition in the midst of noise. There was a time when I believed intuition had no place in research, but lucky for me, Valerie Janesick, my mentor and dissertation chair, opened my eyes to its usefulness. She explained that there is head knowing and heart knowing, and wisdom comes from accessing both.

Like Valerie, writer and researcher for Forbes Women Renee Goyeneche suggests using both the head and the heart in decision-making. When we approach a problem with our heads, we activate our conscious minds and proceed in a logical sequence. We gather information, seek advice, and carefully weigh the options. A logical approach to decision-making is useful, but advice-seeking can get us stuck. When we don't know what to do, it's tempting to ask everyone, from pastors to parents, what path we should take. But too much advice can be overwhelming, especially when it's contradictory, and more importantly, too much advice can keep us from tapping into our own inner knowing.

Heart knowing, on the other hand, can defy logic. Even when all the facts and advice point us one way, our hearts may point us in a different direction. We sometimes call it a "gut feeling," but this knowing comes from our subconscious minds. Heart knowing isn't based solely on emotions, it's based on a lifetime of information and patterns our brains have been filing away for such a time as this. According to Goyeneche, this heart knowing (or intuition) exists for everyone, but some of us are better at accessing it. If we pay attention to our physical cues, we can decide what feels better or worse in our bodies, what makes us feel heavier or lighter. Taking a break from distractions in this empty classroom was allowing me to organize the contents of my head onto the whiteboard and check with my heart to see what felt right.

Should I Stay or Should I Go?

Researcher Deborah Loewenberg Ball once counted a teacher making 20 decisions in about a minute and a half of teaching, and some of those decisions were weighty. Deciding how to respond to a student's unexpected question or challenging behavior can potentially strengthen or harm that student's sense of belonging in the classroom community. Teaching has always been laden with consequential decisions. But lately, teachers across the country have been struggling with one particularly heavy decision: Should I keep teaching, or should I quit? I have lost count of the number of times a teacher has asked me for advice around that question. I would never even begin to counsel someone on something so personal, but I do share some questions teachers can ask themselves when struggling with that decision:

Why did you start teaching, and are those reasons still important to you?
What are the challenges leading you to consider leaving, and are they temporary or long-term?

What are the costs of staying, and what are the costs of leaving?

There are costs either way. Those who choose to stay may sacrifice time and energy for their own families and well-being. And those who choose to go may give up the satisfaction of impacting the lives of young people. In other words, it's a decision that involves both the head and the heart.

Although the challenges of teaching seem more complex and more difficult than ever before, I have to believe that better outcomes can result from our struggling with those challenges. Thich Nhat Hanh, an activist and author, is known for saying "No mud, no lotus." Without suffering through the mud, we cannot find the beauty of the lotus. But this monk and spiritual leader also believes that when we know how to suffer, we suffer less. When we're doing work as complex and difficult as teaching, there will be mud with all its discomfort and messiness. Because struggling doesn't feel good, we try to run away from it or distract ourselves from it. But unless we're able to pause and feel it, we can't use it to create a richer and more fulfilling life. Put simply: when we avoid the difficult stuff, we miss the good stuff. The stories in my data (now spread in stacks across the tables) are full of teachers who were presented with a problem, danced with discomfort, and ended up experiencing the joy of impacting another and the satisfaction of their own growth.

Keep Going

I'm always changed by my research projects and my findings, but nothing has changed me more than embracing pausing, pondering, and persisting. When work responsibilities and expectations start to feel overwhelming, I pause. When I feel frustrated, I stop the snowballing of unhelpful emotions and return to peace. And when something wonderful happens, I pause to savor it. I take in the good feelings instead of just quickly moving on. The curious stance of pondering has also served me well. Cultivating an awareness of the assumptions I make and the biases I carry (about myself and others) takes away invented limitations. Pausing and pondering are simple but not easy. As any new practices, they only become habitual through persistence. And persistence helps me keep the promises I make to myself. I've always prioritized the needs and wants of others, but I haven't always upheld commitments to my own goals and dreams. Persisting in pursuit of greater impact in my work and satisfaction in my life has given me clarity and direction. Quick fixes are rare in teaching and in life. More often, improvement is a long and winding road.

It had been a year since I first met Marcus volunteering at the food bank, a year since he shared his gratitude for Mrs. Pope. It was his story that led to my investigation of pausing, pondering, and persisting, and I think his story will always be my favorite example of the power of this framework. When Mrs. Pope told students they could each have one cookie, Marcus defied her directive and put three more in his pocket. Clearly, situations like these elicit frustration and anger in teachers. It's natural to feel disrespected when students ignore our directions. But Mrs. Pope didn't let those feelings lead her to a an emotionally charged reaction. Instead, she paused. She also pushed aside any assumptions about her student's intentions or character, and she pondered. She asked a question, "Are you hungry?" And Marcus's answer gave her the information she needed to turn that challenging situation into an opportunity for impact.

I've often imagined what would have happened if Mrs. Pope let her emotions take over, if she'd lashed out with harsh words. What if she let her assumptions about Marcus' behavior drive her decision-making? She might have written an office referral or excluded a hungry kid. But she didn't. She paused, pondered, and persisted. She responded thoughtfully and with compassion, and in doing so, changed the trajectory of a young man's life. And since Marcus shared the story with me, Mrs. Pope has impacted my life. She's become a model for the kind of teacher (and person) I want to be. I wonder how many times I've missed an opportunity (or made a situation worse) by reacting in haste. Now that I know better, I'm determined to do better.

Although she's since passed, I have to believe Mrs. Pope found deep satisfaction in turning that challenging moment with Marcus into an opportunity for impact. I hope this book and this work honors her, and the many teachers like her who shape the lives of young people. And I hope it affirms for you, dear reader, how much your work matters. You may not always see the evidence of your impact, but let me assure you, you make a difference in your students' lives in countless ways every day. I hope the practices of pausing, pondering, and persisting help you stay longer, grow stronger, and find even more joy in teaching.

Leveraging the Power of Pausing, Pondering, and Persisting

Pause

Pausing is the first step in turning challenges into opportunities for impact. It requires staying present and cultivating awareness of yourself and of others. When a challenging situation happens in the classroom, notice what you are feeling. Is your heart beating faster? Are your muscles tensing? When you feel this rising tension in your body, take a breath. Try repeating a calming phrase. Give yourself some space before reacting. Over time, you may notice a pattern in the stimuli that precede unhelpful emotions. Knowing yourself and practicing pausing can prevent regrettable reactions.

Ponder

Once you've paused and thwarted a reaction, you can ponder the thoughts tied to your emotions. Are you making assumptions about someone's intentions? Push aside those assumptions in favor of a curious stance. Ask questions from a place of humility and genuine curiosity. Use the information you glean to decide the next right action. Pondering is the key to responding thoughtfully and productively to a challenge.

Persist

Most challenges in teaching (and in life) aren't quickly resolved. More often, you take one step forward and two steps back. Much of teaching is trial and error. But if you can persist over time, you can make a lasting impact on students' lives and facilitate your own growth. Impacting others and growing yourself leads to greater satisfaction. Consistently practicing the three-step framework of pausing, pondering, and persisting is the path to turning challenges into opportunities.

Questions for Reflection

When do you find yourself tempted to react in the classroom? How can knowing yourself help you prevent emotional reactions?

When you find yourself feeling frustrated or angry, what thoughts are you typically thinking? How can you move from unhelpful thoughts to curiosity?

When do you find yourself struggling to persist? How can you give yourself the care and resources needed to persist through challenges?

How will you use the three-step framework of pausing, pondering, and persisting to make a greater impact and find more satisfaction in teaching?

Notes and Works Cited

Spielberger, C. D., Krasner, S. S., & Solomon, E. P. (1988). The experience, expression, and control of anger. In M. P. Janisse (Ed.), *Individual differences, stress, and health psychology: Contributions to psychology and medicine*. Springer.

Kashdan, T. (2009). *Curious? Discover the missing ingredient to a fulfilling life*. William Morrow & Co.

Koren, S. (1997). *Seinfeld: Season 9 Episode 3*. NBC.

Goyeneche, R. (2020). *How to harness intuition and make better decisions*. Forbes Women,: August 31, 2020.

Lowenberg, D. B. (2018). *Just dreams and imperatives: The power of teaching in the struggle for public education.* Annual Presidential Address at the American Educational Research Association. Retrieved from https://www.youtube.com/watch?v=JGzQ7O_SIYY&feature=youtu.be&t=35m26s

Nhat Hạnh, T., & Morphew, J. (2014). *No mud, no lotus: the art of transforming suffering.* Parallax Press.

Epilogue

After more than six years of collecting teacher impact stories, The Chalk and Chances project continues to evolve. The Chalk and Chances website (chalkandchances.com) is the place to find the stories, and the collection is updated each week. You'll also find resources to help you turn challenges into opportunities for impact on the website. I am blessed to give talks and presentations about the project to audiences around the world, and you can check out my TEDx Talk (titled The Teachers We Remember) on YouTube. The best part of sending this book out into the world is the opportunity to connect with readers like you. I treasure your thoughts and your feedback. You can engage in the conversation through social media using the hashtag #PausePonderPersist. Or, you can engage with me directly on Twitter and Instagram, @JulieSHasson.

I have been blessed to be in the company of so many amazing teachers throughout this journey. Although you and I may never meet in person, I want to thank you for the difference you make in the lives of others. Your effort to turn challenges into opportunities for impact leaves ripples of goodness in the world. Keep going and know that I am here, cheering for you.

DOI: 10.4324/9781003344735-13

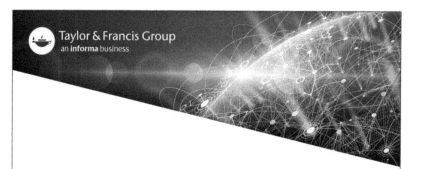

For Product Safety Concerns and Information please contact our EU
representative GPSR@taylorandfrancis.com
Taylor & Francis Verlag GmbH, Kaufingerstraße 24, 80331 München, Germany

www.ingramcontent.com/pod-product-compliance
Ingram Content Group UK Ltd.
Pitfield, Milton Keynes, MK11 3LW, UK
UKHW021447080625
459435UK00012B/398